"Surviving the War
Against Yourself"

Thomas and Amber Dunning

Cover design by Daniel Hill

Contents

Dedication

This book is dedicated to William "Will" Bonner.

Thomas & Amber Dunning

Acknowledgements

We'd like to give our unending love and gratitude to our parents: Lee, Rach, Deborah, Dave, Roger, Fiona and our brothers, sisters, grandparents, in-laws and cousins, aunts and uncles, nieces and nephews as well as all our extended family for all of their support throughout our journey. For sitting with us for hours on end in A&E, booking us flights so you could take care of us, for all the guidance and advice and for being the best family we could wish for.

We would also like to thank all of our friends and colleagues, but especially: Julie, Lisa, Josh, Dave, Billy and Darren who stuck by us during the darkest days, dried countless tears, made us laugh when we needed it most and never asked for anything in return.

To all the team behind TEDx Brayford Pool, thank you for being the first to believe in our story, for giving us the platform to share it, for the guidance, coaching and for being the most amazing surrogate family.

We would like to thank Taryn Johnston and the team at Chronos Publishing for making this book happen and for not only taking the time to understand us as a couple and our story but also for helping us to share it in a way that was authentic and honest. We knew from the moment we sat down for that first coffee with you that no one else could do our journey justice like you have.

Finally, to you, the reader. This book is for you.
We hope that by sharing our story we can give you hope that no matter what, things can get better. The road to recovery is far from easy, but we hope that whether you're living with mental illness yourself, or caring for someone who is, you will find your light at the end of the tunnel.

Foreword by Richard Askam
Speaker, Writer, Broadcaster

"Holding on to anger is like drinking poison and hoping it kills somebody else."

It's a great quote which I have used several times in various speeches but never been quite clear who to attribute it to. It feels like a misquote of a similar line from Nelson Mandela, which he didn't write either but did make famous:

"Resentment is like drinking poison and waiting for your enemy to die."

I love these sort of epiphany phrases because, as a speaker, it allows you to make a clear point to your audience of the power of re-invention and the mythical currency of inspiration that flows from that.

For me, the joy of being a public speaker is only matched by coaching others to become better at being a public speaker. Young or old, educated or not – most of us where born with the ability to speak to each other but in recent years, we have lost the feeling of necessity to speak to each other.

I blame Steve Jobs for letting people talk through pocket size keyboards using only their thumbs.

The very action of holding a conversation, often with strangers, has a hugely therapeutic value, often to both parties – which is why we somehow feel better about our problems by airing them first, then addressing them second.

Once that threshold has been crossed – the strength that comes from that allows you to start climbing back up the hill of life.

I met Thomas & Amber in 2018, I was coaching Thomas for his TEDx Youth event. We had several rehearsals and from the moment he started to talk so eloquently and frankly about his experiences detailed in this book, I was hooked. Their story of climbing up the hill together is as compelling as it is extraordinary, the fact they have both written it from their own perspectives is genius.

Enjoy…

Chapter 1 - A Shot across the bow (T)

It was primary school, ages four through eleven. It was here that I was to encounter the first of what was to become a daily occurrence of bullying and abuse. I was to be isolated from the other children and tormented about my weight, brought to tears by the mercilessness of the playground bullies, those who had a thirst for abusing the ones they considered weak and easy prey.

Okay so maybe that was "a bit too" strong; I mean we were kids at the end of the day, but those memories are branded in my mind, clear and ever present. There were only really ever two friends which stick out in my primary school journey, and that would be Josh and Michael.

Josh was exactly like me, we both got bullied most of the time together as a pair, but with the similar interests of popular culture at the time for four year olds. Power rangers was the latest craze alongside *Tazos*, *Pogs*, *yo-yos* and then by year six when we were 100 years old – *Pokémon* hit the playground.

Michael and I might as well have been stuck together! Most Fridays we would be staying at each-others houses for a sleepover, going to the youth club or just playing video games. Thankfully Michael lived on the local Royal Airforce base where I was living, for a few hundred metres I was safe until he walked in his front door. Then came the impossible task of sprinting home to evade my pursuers.

Every break, lunchtime and on the walk home, we would always be together; we were all best mates. As I look back now, *and yes hindsight is a wonderful thing*, I realise that at age nine, a catalyst of this friendship would trigger what was to be the first step of my future mental health journey.

Michael was leaving.

He was changing schools which would leave just me and Josh. That wasn't the issue and being just the two of us wasn't the problem, even though Josh was making friends of his own. That was and still is to this day fine by me. The thing was, me and Michael were always that constant, like brothers almost.

Every Friday like clockwork we would go to the local youth club, me staying close just in case I was targeted, and then we'd stay at either one's house. The time came where he cleared out his drawer in the classroom for the last time and I had to say goodbye.

The next day he was gone.

The next few weeks were turbulent, to say the least. I was starting to act out, not only at home but at school. I became aggressive and was unable to concentrate.

I often felt persecuted by teachers for picking on me when I was in my own little world, to be fair they were probably just making sure I was listening. Feeling persecuted didn't really bode well for me, I genuinely thought that the teachers were on the side of the bullies; this suffering did not have any end in sight; there was no escape! It would then escalate to me screaming at the teachers in front of the class and then either throwing a chair or picking up a table, before storming out.

Looking back, I can hear the echoes of this time reverberating in my head. As if I were time traveller gone back to relive a life, just to try to make sense or to even change the story

"*You're one of them miss; you're no better.*"

A statement from a nine-year-old me. She replies "*I've tried to stop them for you!*"

"*Yeah, well they're still doing it aren't they.*" I fired back.

Just like that; I was sent to isolation for the entire week. From what I heard at the time, there was talk of me being moved classrooms as understandably she felt she couldn't teach or control me. Of course, she was not on their side, but right there and then what else could I have done?

It seemed evident to me that everyone was against me and I had no hope.

At this moment in time, I didn't care what anyone said.

This wasn't me at all!

I remember one specific day where a teacher came into class and said he needed a word. Mr Bland; the teacher everyone wanted. Not too strict but knew how to make the school experience enjoyable for all, also introduced us to my favourite poet Michael Rosen, who remains so to this very day.

Thinking I was going to be in the headmaster's office, I edged out with my tail between my legs expecting the worst; but what actually happened was completely different. We literally walked around the school grounds when he asked me "*Is everything alright?*" little did I know in this moment; this question would then follow me through my life.

This was the first time where rather than being excluded from the classroom to work on my own, someone actually took an interest in me. Was this the first shot across the bow?

The eerie sense of foreboding sits strong in me whenever I think back to this date and if only, I could see what was going on and spoke out; maybe EVERYTHING could have been sidestepped and avoided?

This was also where my curse got hold. I replied – *"Nothing, I'm okay sir."* Again, a statement which would follow me though for years to come.
I couldn't tell the truth.

I'd tried speaking to a teacher before but the consequences of this action saw me covered head to toe in bruises and my brain scared with even more mental torment.

After all, it was my belief that the teachers were on the side of the bullies, why would this one be any different?

It was at this age where I would have to sprint home to avoid the devilish pursuit of those bullying me, and given my size (Yep, I was the physical metaphor of the fat kid in school), I would inevitably fail to get away.

Because of the failing of what is now the first rule of "zombieland" – Cardio - I'd be thrown to the floor; punched, kicked and of course have the verbal abuse thrown at me. I would then get home to be covered in mud, grass stains and then to wrap it all off I would lie to my mum and dad and tell them that I was just playing football at lunchtime. This was the exact same "go-to" excuse for my body being covered in the marks and brands of the bullies. We were children after all and we ran around, they wouldn't expect a thing.

I would like to stress at this point, my parents are absolutely incredible; they were always supportive, loving and caring. They were not to know I was being bullied to the extent I was; even growing up with two older brothers, they never really knew the gravitas of the situation.

Everything that I've mentioned was a daily occurrence. A tormented reality which would be the foundations which my mental illness in future years would be built on.

One lunchtime – Year six / eleven years old – I'd had enough. It was this year where the school was trialling the new system of having half the school kids in for one half of lunch while the other half were outside. Naturally, with my great amount of luck, I was with those who gave me a good kicking on the way home from school. "*Ahh but it's alright, you had Josh, didn't you?*" I'm guessing you're thinking to yourself. Nope. He was in the other half.

It almost feels like it was planned, of course, it was most likely simply the luck of the draw or some register scheme. To me, it felt like a sick, twisted Key Stage Two gauntlet had been thrown down.

For anyone who's a fan of the Saw movies, right now "*Do you want to play a game?*" would sum up how I felt that very first lunchtime.

I was lured into playing a game of football and I genuinely thought I was making friends. What a sigh of relief that I was being accepted, I was almost normal; almost human and that everything that had gone before was now over.

I was wrong.

Lured on false pretences, we went to the furthest part of the field, and once we got kicked off – it literally kicked off. I was pushed around, thrown to the floor and what can only be described as a tsunami of hatred started to drown me. Being encircled with no way out and essentially in a pit of pure despair. I just laid there hoping that just like a pack of hyena's they would get bored and move onto their next prey.

This isn't the end, however. Something came over me, I'd had enough. I sprinted to the nearest classroom. Stood in front of everyone and screamed *"Who else wants to have a go at me!"* with tears bowling down my face.

Not the outcome I'd expected. In my head, I thought they would say *"Oh, are you okay? Do you need help?"* but how wrong could I have been!
I spent the next week in isolation, in the school's staff room - for my own safety… Wicked!

Going off-piste for a bit, let's go back to feeling targeted by my class teacher. I'm sure, it was probably because they thought I wasn't listening and the reality was, I quite simply wasn't. However, the only time where this was a problem in my life was on a Wednesday. I would be suddenly struck down with an illness, in fact, you could put a confident bet on me being off with "illness" on a Wednesday.

This was a very specific day and I'm pretty sure you're asking yourself "Why Wednesday?"

Wednesday was the day of English comprehension study; not exactly the worse subject in the world, but when you're in the same room as all those who bully you for half a day, you feel a certain level of stress, that you're locked in a cage with what were essentially predators; in fact, they're not that good; looking back I would happily say they were feral. I wouldn't be poorly in the slightest. I was starting to play truant as a way to keep myself isolated and away from that environment. Back at home, there was only really one person who picked up on this. Will.

If you recall, I previously mentioned that I grew up with two older brothers. Will and Rob – Rob, nine years older and Will, seven years older than me, so yep I was definitely the baby of the three of us.
Will and I never really saw eye to eye, we would fight and scrap but behind the facade, you could tell he loved me as his brother.

Out of the blue, Will eventually asked me:
"Why Wednesday?"
"What do you mean?" I replied with a level of anxiety.
"Why is it you're always ill on a Wednesday?"

Well, that was it, I broke down into tears and told him everything. How I was chased home, how I was bullied, how I was essentially assaulted for a group's sickening pleasure.

That was the moment it changed. Me and Will never fought again – it was quite the opposite.

I came home after being beaten one specific afternoon, telling mum and dad the usual lie of "Football practice". Will shot out the front door, leaving behind the metaphorical, cartoonist smoke trail as he took off down the road to find the perpetrators. I never felt this outside of the house before.

I felt safe.

Chapter 2 – From strong Foundations. (T)

This went on for YEARS.

Secondary school pretty much came and went, same usual outcome; beaten up, bullied, made a few friends but most of the time I just wanted to seclude myself away. The biggest change came when Rob joined the RAF and Will joined the British Army. Although they were in contact quite often, I felt unprotected again, but this time it was slightly different, I actually had some friends. A close group where we looked after each other and who I could put some faith in. Josh... you know that one from chapter one, ended up coming to the same secondary school, finally - I was way overdue some luck!

He was that guy, the one I could rely on and we both always knew when something was wrong. We weren't as close but we didn't have to be, it was one of those friendships where we didn't have to be around each other 24/7. I had two or three friends who were in my form who have pretty much stayed close all the way though so that definitely was a plus!

The continuation of bullying saw me getting targeted while lining up, waiting for lessons to start. Walking down the tight corridors of the school buildings gave them opportunity to punch me in the gut, many times while just walking from lesson to lesson; and then that's when the first signs of depression started to emerge.

I was 14 years old when finally, it all became too much.

After the daily abuse on the bus home I remember just thinking
"That's it, I'm going end this."

That evening I stayed in my room all night. On my bed, surrounded with every medication which was in the house.

Paracetamol & Ibuprofen – Random family prescriptions.

It got to the point where I dressed in clean clothes so it would be less effort for the "Aftercare" for want of a better word and I was ready; sat waiting for the moment where I prayed for my head to enter auto-pilot and just take the tablets to end the suffering.

Instead of this auto pilot, my head went into a state which I can only describe as "last chance survival" where I could do nothing but think of all those people I would be leaving behind – Mum, Dad, Will, Rob, Josh…

In an absolute state of tears and exhaustion, I took all the medications back downstairs, put it all away, back in their places so no one could tell they had ever been moved. I didn't tell anyone what I was about to do because I just knew it would cause more issues at school. The problems with education then started again; although being present in the room, I really struggled with certain lessons and couldn't get involved. I became an introvert almost overnight.

Before this became such a huge problem, I did seek help with the school councillor team about what was going on and more specifically what happened but it was put down to the best excuse someone who is 14 years old can be given.

"You're going through changes [Puberty] and this is normal for someone your age."

My feelings and thoughts not considered at all. What was the point? Even the school Councillor wasn't interested!

The bullying came to an end in year 10. Well, I say an end, the frequency reduced but was still ever present.

It was a lunchtime on just the average school day. I was sat in my usual place and some of those people who previously went out of their way to bring me down were just beside me. I can't remember fully how the conversation went but all I remember was I had enough. This auto-pilot which I wanted to kick in when I wanted to put a full stop on my life, now decided it wanted to have some fun. My clenched fist, which I wanted to be as dense as concrete, swung across the bully's face – It felt good! But this is where it all started to get scary - Everything was in slow motion.

This was pay back.

I didn't want to hurt him.

I wanted him dead.

Something had control of me and I could do nothing but watch. Given the history, there was no way I was going to interfere; I wouldn't be able even if I wanted to! If I couldn't take my own life, I for once wanted to take control of it.

While everything was in slow motion, two dinner ladies were running to break the fight up, but of course this then gives me one hell of a weird memory.

I don't know what dinner ladies were like in your school either now or back when you were that age, but imagine them in Baywatch but replace Pamela Anderson with that thought; Yep, I'll leave that one with you!

They came and grabbed me by the wrists to stop me swinging and trying to chase down my target which worked for all of about two minutes; he came back and taunted me. I managed to slip my wrists out of their grip and then the chase continued. It didn't really come to a stop until roughly three people held on each arm trying to hold me back and I physically tired out. But mind you, at 6ft and eighteen stone, it took some doing – I was only fourteen years old so I was a fairly big guy still.

I was ushered away and taken straight to the headmaster's office like I was the culprit; like I was the one who was at fault; like I was the one who had committed a crime.

I was sat in a chair, awaiting my fate. "*What have I done?*" I kept saying to myself. "*What was that?*" I wondered. The very same councillor whom I had only seen a few weeks previously came over to me with a clip board and a pen. She took one look at me and said "*Fill this out.*"

No sooner had she appeared; she had walked away. She must have known if something was done, said or even acknowledged when I saw her previously; this may have not happened – the way she just appeared and went again suggests she must have known this.

The headmaster's door swung open. And there stood the frame of the judge, jury and executioner.

There are numerous things I'll take to the grave with me, the first one was Mr. Bland from about five or six years previous, the next one is that of the headmaster Mr. Elms –

"This isn't like you is it boy!"

"No sir..."

Because I was seen as the perpetrator to this, I was labelled as the aggressor and given a suspension until the end of the week. Somehow nearly overnight in the school's eyes I was not a danger to myself, but a danger to other pupils. Was anyone even listening to me?!

I felt awful. Not because of the fight, if anything I was proud of myself for the first time in my life, that I protected myself and didn't take any more abuse off people; I was scared. I was scared of myself, of the pure fact that if I really could have, I would have done far worse than just a punch across the face. I wanted him dead and I wanted to do it as bad as a shark that's got the first sniff of blood.

The days I had off I was given homework and also grounded by my parents; in fact, I remember my mother saying

"Obviously your grounded and you understand it was the wrong thing to do ... but I am so proud of you for standing up for yourself."

Another quote that will go down with me through history. The grounding was not really a punishment; I hardly left the house to begin with so it would have been worse if I hadn't been!

When I returned back on the Monday, I was ready to get back to some form of normality. Even though I still don't feel like it was all my fault for this fight, I still felt a great deal of remorse and shame for my actions. Like the headmaster said, this wasn't like me at all. The school knew this and well to be honest; from my own point of view it seemed like the school did not have a clue what to do with me.

As soon as I set foot onto the school ground, I was ushered into the head of year's office where my mum was also waiting. I couldn't help but have the subtle hint of paranoia and suspense envelop me like a blanket of emotion. Turns out that the school wouldn't let me return to classes unless one of the two conditions were met:

1. <u>I have a councillor with me in every lesson</u>

Learning wasn't the problem, in fact where I was in lessons with those who had the sick perversion in making my life hell, I just got on with my work. I mean; to be honest, I didn't really get involved in lessons much but I got the work done at least. At this point in time mum actually trained people who could have potentially been doing that role in the care of myself; not a chance was I going to allow this. How humiliating it would have been if I'd had someone as my learning councillor that my mother had trained; not a chance I was going to let that happen.

2. <u>Have anger management counselling during lunch time.</u>

I suppose this was the better of the two deals, but looking at it, it's like being offered a choice between either gonorrhoea or syphilis. I couldn't take the first offer because like I said, no way I'm putting mum through that, so me being me, I took the second option. Receive Anger Management counselling which I didn't need (Or did I? I don't know now really) and sacrifice one lunch time a week.

On a personal note; this was the first time where I was actually scared of myself so maybe this could be where my life "should" have turned around.

Life was now about to change but before I go any further, all of you beautiful people reading who are either in some form of education or work and go through bullying of this calibre; getting into a fight IS NOT the right way to go about it!

Okay, lets continue.

Chapter 3 – The popular years. (T)

It's Year Ten, I'm now back at school following the fight and well things have drastically changed. You haven't missed a few pages and I've not missed anything from the end of chapter two, but the difference is comparable to night and day.

Monday morning and the day where I return to school. I step out of the head of years office and tentatively walk across the school grounds into my first lesson of the day – English.

I was in the bottom set of English and with students who were all mates with the person who I hit, and also with those who took pleasure in making my life hell; and tattooing my arms, legs and torso in bruises.

"Hi, Tom!" "Welcome back mate!" "Hope you're okay!"

"...Uh, hello?" – the confusion being evident in my response.

Somehow, these people were now taking an interest in me, it was only a small group of students and a teacher who in all honesty deserved to be teaching a more, higher level of English and took great interest in making sure we all did the work, concentrated and also ensured we enjoyed the classroom – Another teachers name etched onto the memory muscle of the brain, "Mrs Burr".

Up to the end of the week where we all had English again, we actually all meshed and became great friends. I was a big guy still at this point and because of this, I was branded with a nickname. Looking back, it was kind of cruel but I actually found it funny and enjoyed it, "Mr Kipling" – and yes, that's after the cake baker. I finally felt accepted.

This classroom now felt like a family and one where I felt an ounce of safety. I had people who are now taking an active interest in me, and even a teacher who you could just tell wanted the best out of all of us – and this was only the first lesson of the day!

"Welcome back Tom!"

"Good to see you mate!"

"TOM!!"

Students all over the school knew who I was. I wasn't being threatened; wasn't being antagonised; I was being welcomed!

I gained more friends and started to get up in the morning looking forward to the place where I actually called and referred to as "hell." It was such a great place to be and I felt loved. This popularity saw me invited to parties, invited to events, and people even wanted me to join them on the way to classes! This is where another individual of my story comes in, the person who would later on in my life not only be my flatmate, but also my best man – "Billy."

Billy has a love of media. Video games, movies, TV series, the lot. In fact, many years later when we lived together, we had to spend £120 on five DVD racks for his PlayStation and Xbox games alongside his library of Blu-ray and DVDs! We connected over the love of this, but also for the love of music; and one track in particular by "The Who".

In GCSE science we sat together and we would have one headphone in each ear. We would cram the music volume up as loud as we could and then something happened which has never happened since Josh and I were younger playing pretend power rangers.

Billy and I entered a realm of imagination – we were the best Air guitar, Air keyboard and Air drummers in the damn world!

Eyes closed while the lines for the track "Baba O'Riley" blared out *"Its only teenage wasteland"* we would start to sing and get so far into it that I would open my eyes to see the entire class of 30 pupils and Mr Beacock staring point blank at us.

"Uhhh Billy..." - I said, trying to get his attention.

"SALLY TAKE MY HAND!" – Billy burst into song.

Only giving Billy a shove on the shoulder would he then open his eyes. We both sat there looking at everyone in stunned silence.

"...Sorry sir."- we both said in unison, red-faced.

This is just one example but we had many more moments like this and from it, school went fast; scary fast. Moments which I wanted to hold onto forever, fell through the fingertips of time like sand in the palm of a three-year-old.

GCSE exams came and went and I didn't really suffer from any sign of mental illness or distress yet – not even a warning shot like back in year Ten and the fight which turned my school life around. Billy and I went onto sixth form where we would both unknowingly study psychology together and become almost inseparable. We started to make movies and video blogs together. We even set up our own production groups, "Bojangles On The Wall Entertainment" was Billy's and mine was "BIGtom Productions". We would have a bit of friendly competition on how many YouTube views we could get – In fact as a side note, I'm pretty sure if you YouTube either of those, you'll get the original videos we made back in 2007 – 2008! As you can tell, things got good and as I said, the difference was night and day. From being chased home and assaulted and the first attempt to take my own life; to now having lifelong friends, being socially accepted in school and well – Simply enjoying every day possible.

It was the second year of 6th form, I dropped a subject and started to continue with my A-levels. My life was about to change forever.

I associated myself with a small group of people in the common room who were all taking Btec Drama – I was the odd one out as I was studying Physics, electronics and resistant materials but one day I had to come in with more baggage than that of just my laptop, folder and pencil case.

The night before this baggage was forced upon me, Mum wanted to speak to me but in my room. I thought mum may have found the lads mags under my bed and well, it was either going to be "the talk" OR "you're grounded."

Mum was sat on my bed with her head in her hands. *"Yep, she had definitely found the magazines,"* I thought. My heart started to race and the colour drained from my face when I tentatively walked over to mum. I could her hear sobbing, I sat beside her, put my arm around her and asked what was wrong.

"Will's coming home!" – she said while trying to stifle her emotions.

This was when the Iraq war was going on and Will was out there with the army playing soldiers.

"Get in! but surely that's a good thing?" I replied.

I'll never forget the calm of how mum spoke when she answered; the still of the air and how time just stood still.

"Will has Cancer Tom."

Time was frozen. No thoughts came in or went out of my head. This person who I regarded as invincible, as heroic as Marvel's Captain America has got a condition which, well let's face it; all you can think about is the most negative outcome – almost as if it's the one-way ticket on the high-speed train to the afterlife.

This was a new battle which I now had to contend with. On a selfish note, I'd always relied on Will, what was I going to do now? He needed me more than ever but was I even strong enough without his help? Throughout the first chapters of my life, he had played such a significant part in helping to look after me and now I needed to be strong and repay the favour with interest.

This was now the little brother's time to shine.

Chapter 4 – Years of deep regret. (T)

The foundation of support that Will provided was now receiving huge tremors; the very fabric of self-respect, courage and sense of humour was now taking a battering and in that awkward phase of stability only described as "Will it or won't it go?"

This was all going on around me and I was in the sixth form doing my A-levels at the time. I couldn't really make sense of it all because in a matter of twenty-four hours the tables, had turned massively. I had absolutely no idea how to be supportive, I'd always relied on those around me to do that for me so I guess I now had to learn.

I couldn't bear the thought of Will suffering with what he was going through; I left the sixth form, I stayed at a part-time job where I earned £189 a month, this was barely enough to keep me and the moped on the road, never mind paying my keep to my parents.

Mum would come into my room and ask:
"We're going to see Will. Are you coming?"
"No sorry I can't, I've got course work to get on with"
I would flat out lie to my parents who still believed I was actually in education when I wasn't. Instead, my parents would go to Nottingham to see him in hospital while I was sat at home, playing video games on my own; disassociating with the world to prevent any acknowledgement of my own feelings.

This went on for months. I'm pretty sure I completed *Final Fantasy XII* at least three times over, did the extra quests and exhausted everything I could do on the multiple playthroughs; Until one day.

I owned up to my parents and then the next time they went down to see Will it was after his six sessions of chemotherapy. I was a rubbish brother, never mind trying to pay back all the help and protection he gave me over the years.

This wasn't the appointment where I should have started to see him. The Cancer had started in his foot and to give you a comparison of what it looked like, it appeared to be a golf ball-sized lump under his skin but just sat there as a harbinger of what devastating outcome could just be around the corner.

This was the day where I also saw him cry for the first time, ever; I genuinely thought this man was incapable and lacked tear ducts up until this day.

It was broken to us that there were no more possible treatments going forward and the cancer was still as aggressive as the first day; it had also spread to his lungs. The news that no doctor ever wants to give their patient:

"The cancer is terminal."

For about ten, possibly fifteen minutes there was not a dry eye in the room and understandably mum had Will in her arms. This day will forever be etched on my memory for two things: the first one is obvious. No one wants to hear that their brother or son is going to die and within a time frame.

The second one always brings a smile to my face and a memory of how I will always remember my fallen hero. He told mum point blank to her face something which all us brothers and dad all kept secret.

Mum is a proud Cornish lady; she made the most incredible pasties and everything by hand. The filling was absolutely out of this world; it was the perfect Cornish pasty outside of Cornwall; however, the pastry was like eating gypsum. With every tantalising bite, the filling lured you into a false sense of security while the pastry held the dirty secret of requiring a small reservoir of water to even think about swallowing.

On this day, the day where Will was told the cancer had won, he said with a smile on his face:

"Mum, when I'm gone promise me one thing."

"...Okay" replied mum.

"Change your bloody pastry recipe. It's like eating talc!"

Everyone immediately stopped crying and all jaws just hit the floor with a "I CAN'T BELIEVE HE JUST SAID THAT!!"

In the coming months, Will went ahead and planned his wedding to my now sister-in-law Fran.

I wanted to make my brother proud so I applied for an apprenticeship as a mechanical engineer. I was eventually invited for an interview. I felt like I had aced it so in all the excitement I phoned Will and told him the great news.

"I'm proud of you mate." – he said.

Five little words never meant so much to me before this.

This now takes us up to the inevitability of Will's passing.

We were all staying in a hotel for a family celebration when without any warning, life would use its ability to be completely irrational and unpredictable like a child passing through the toddler years.

While getting changed, Will succumbed to his illness and died a few hours later. Mum was the one who had to break the news to me after witnessing the horrors no mother should ever have to see.

She was in pieces and told me to go to my hotel room while she spoke to Rob - something had definitely happened. I complied and tentatively went up to the room thinking Will was okay and just wanted to see us. Opening the door slowly I could see no one there but the girlfriend I was with at the time, waiting for me on the edge of the bed. I sat beside her, said nothing and just kept talking to myself in my head. Mum came in through the door with Rob and Dad – I instantly knew the worst news possible would be true. I bolted for the door. *"If they didn't tell me what I did not want to hear, it wouldn't be true!"* my deluded mind told me in pure desperation. Rob grabbed me and got me to sit on the bed with mum. Mum told me there and then that Will had died. It was almost like Will set out on his goal, that he was going to get married, and that smile which haunts me to this day was him saying *"I've got married, it's now time for me to go"*

I don't really remember much past this day for about a week after. The funeral came about quite quickly and when the day of the actual funeral came, we were able to see him in the chapel of rest.

This was entirely new to me and was such a foreign concept my brain felt like it had shut down. Mum pulled me to one side before we walked into the funeral director's office and gave me a crash course about what was about to happen. I was told we could see Will one last time and that made my psyche create a delusion that this was all a hidden camera show. I just nodded at everything mum was saying and I was genuinely looking around for cameras. *"This can't be real"* I kept telling myself.

We lined up on the side of the room where Will was resting, I couldn't really fathom what was going on, so little but so much was going on around me, my brain was shrugging its metaphorical shoulders trying to figure out what to do.

Before we went in, Fran and Rob went to pay their respects, giving Will a kiss on the cheek just before leaving. Then it was my turn. Again, I really don't remember much except just staring at Will and begging for this all to be a sick elaborate joke. Mum gave Will a kiss on the cheek leaving behind a tear. It looked as if Will was definitely putting it on and was starting to cry because the joke was going too far.

This wasn't a joke. No matter how long I stared waiting for the faintest of twitches from the body; nothing happened. I left the room knowing this was the last time I would ever see Will again.

I don't quite know why but I have no memory of the funeral. It could be the reason why even now that my head is wanting to protect itself. I wasn't laden with alcohol; I wasn't laden with drugs; I just simply cannot remember.

All I can remember is the fact, pure and simple that I wasn't there for Will. I wasn't there for my brother who did so much to change my life and give me some form of protection. I didn't even wish him a happy birthday thinking it would mean more next year when he was all clear.

This could be the layer of regret that starts to manifest later on in my life.

I had applied for an apprenticeship before Will's wedding and my fate were about to take a weird turn.

The same week after I said my goodbye to Will I received a call from the factory where I had applied for the apprenticeship – I got the job.

Chapter 5 – Things can only get better. (T)

Within the week of the funeral, I was now an employee of a local food factory as a mechanical engineer apprentice, which saw me immediately start my NVQs and my Engineering qualifications, so I didn't really have time to mourn my brother's demise. If history is anything to go by, I couldn't just breakdown into tears and vent my emotions because that's one of the reasons why I got bullied, and why I got chased home only to suffer the inevitable beatings from those cowardly people; especially going into a new college and a new job, I definitely couldn't risk showing my emotions just in case this trauma started again. I did the only thing I could at the time and did what all men are told to do in today's society – Man up, bottle my emotions, toss them aside for another day.

With this fresh bottle of emotions now out of clear sight, I carried on with my life. The year that followed, saw Billy and I get our own flat together near my place of work. It was the first time I had moved out of my parents' house and we spent the next six months in what can only be described as a student cesspit.

We made it our own though! Billy kept us entertained with the world's largest back catalogue of DVD's, video games and the assortment of games consoles he owned and I did most of the cooking. We only stayed here for 6 months until we decided that the flat was actually a really nasty shell of a building and I had things going off at the parent's house.

Mum and Dad were separating for reasons I'm not going to go into here – I mean it's not important for the progression of the book, nor is it my business, but it left Mum on her own.

I came back to help her out and be supportive as she was understandably still raw with emotion over the loss of her middle child. Dad had moved onto the local airbase in the on-site accommodation so I visited him regularly. No matter what happened; mum was always going to be my mum, and dad was always going to be my dad. Understandably, he was also raw with emotions from the passing.

With being back in my hometown I met a new group of friends and we started to become really close. Pretty much every Tuesday, Thursday and Saturday we were guaranteed to be out in town, drinking until we saw double of everything and generally having a laugh. I became this typical "Lad" where I would take people home, get stood up, go out again and the cycle continues.

You would think, a young guy like me at the age of 21 and meeting people, getting drunk and taking people back to his place was living the life that most men only dream of; looking back, this was already a massive warning flag.

This was not me.

Without knowing it, the emotions which I had bottled up had caused me to turn into this overly confident young man, who purposely went out to meet people and as they say "Netflix and Chill." This wasn't me at all. Was this me grieving? My friends saw me as the guy who always met the girls and I was guaranteed to not be going home on my own, or even going back to my place.

I can look back now and laugh thinking "oh yeah I did that" but looking back at it more deeply, I can only think that I was in denial of my own issues and I was subconsciously always trying to keep this "bottle" hidden from the light of day. This was destructive and the worse thing about it, I didn't even see it. I was spiralling, drinking myself silly three nights a week, doing exams and studying and somehow, I was still on track? Two years went by doing this.

While this was going on, on the rare nights where I did not go out, I would stay up until the early hours of the morning either giving lifts to make sure the people I considered family got home okay, or even just to get a text that they were alright.

I even went as far sometimes, to pop to a chain coffee shop (Loads to choose from, but I'll let you make that decision) and buy them breakfast and a coffee to nurse their hangovers. I've never really had a group of friends this close before and I wasn't going to let anything get in the way of that. It's something I always dreamed of as a child growing up.

While I was in a nosedive, I was able to save myself and regain the reigns of control when I actually wanted to settle down and that's when I met the best thing to ever happen to me. I met Amber.

Amber got in contact with me through online dating and in all honesty, it was a medium where I was meeting new people but this time like I said, I wanted to settle down and have a loving relationship. I was sat in my living room ready to go out for the usual binge, the taxi was already called, leaving the house was imminent; but with Amber, there was something strange compared to all the other girls who I had met previously. We had a connection.

The five or ten minutes we spoke were amazing, we had a laugh, got to know each other by breaking the ice and then she said something which to this day we both still laugh about.

"Oh, you know my mate *** don't you!" – this message hit me like a log hitting a freshly cleaned sliding window door.

"Ahh..." I replied. *"Yeah, I do"*

Turns out that this person was the last girl I took home; I had unknowingly slept with Amber's mate previously. As it turns out, she had been singing my praises and that I was a lovely guy and that I was on the dating website which in some really bizarre twist of fate, Amber joined and then by pure luck, we met from there.

As far as when people say "our love was meant to be!" I dare you to go out there and find another true story similar to this!

The taxi arrived shortly later and picked me and my friends up; so Amber and I swapped numbers and that was it, off to the usual nightlife spots and on with the night.

After about a month of talking, Amber had come around to my house. Well, she missed her bus so I had to pick her up, in doing so missing our dinner reservation in town so we sat on top of the hill near my house in the car, stared at the city lights and in the smoothest move I have ever done since Barry white sang *"can't get enough of your love baby"*, put on Ed Sheeran's first album and started to sing it to Amber.

That night I asked if we could make us official and well, that is how we started!

Time went on and Amber changed her application from Sheffield University to where I was living, she got a dorm room in a block of student housing where I wouldn't leave. Not on purpose mind; we ended up "accidentally" living with one another while she attended her course. Since her flat was only a few miles away from my actual house, we stayed at mine for a few nights; within a day her toothbrush was in the bathroom – She was officially starting to move in!

My studies were going really well, I was getting straight distinctions in all my subjects as part of my mechanical engineering courses, work was going incredible and I was happy. Happy on the path life was finally taking me.

And yet out of the blue, something hugely unpredictable would happen next. Before I go on, I must stress; this was possibly one of the happiest five years of my life. I went on without having an ounce of issues from the emotional bottle I had put aside five years previous from Will's funeral; I got my Foundation Degree in mechanical engineering, I had an amazing girlfriend, I had health and also a great group of friends.

The year was now 2013, Almost overnight after I graduated – I became: Introverted. Anxious. Self-destructive.

My life would now be turned upside down.

Chapter 6 – In at the deep end (A)

Falling in love with Tom was a bit of a whirlwind. Within days of our first conversation, we were talking for hours and hours at a time. I would cancel plans just to spend more time on Skype with him and it didn't matter what we talked about, I just found him endlessly fascinating and I knew right then and there, even in those early days, that he was someone I wanted in my life forever.

After a month or so of getting to know each other, we met in person for the first time. I was so relieved that I felt just as comfortable and he was just as attractive, thoughtful and funny in person. In fact, it still makes me smile almost seven years later thinking about the lengths he went to, making sure I had all I needed. He bought me a bottle of water because it was a hot day and lent me his pyjamas when I forgot mine. He'd even bought one of each type of wine just to make sure I had something I liked.

Tom asked me out that very first night, cuddled up on a rug in front of the fire, watching *P.S. I love You.* Romantic, right? Wrong. I ignored his question because my brain was buzzing with excitement and I knew full well the closest thing to a 'yes' I would be able to muster would be some sort of barely audible squeal. So, thankfully not put off, he asked me again a few hours later and I managed to translate my excitement into words this time.

The following day I met his mum who is one of the loveliest, funniest and strongest women I know and immediately felt so warmly welcomed by her and her partner, Dave. Although it might not have been the most traditional start to a relationship, I had never been this sure about anything in all my life. I knew this because for the first time, out of all the relationships I'd been in (not that many, honestly) I actually wanted to tell my family about Tom. I had become used to hiding relationships from my parents as I knew deep down that they wouldn't work out and my Dad definitely wouldn't like them.

Tom was different. I couldn't wait for him to meet my family and desperately hoped they would approve. Thankfully, when the day came, it went without a hitch… apart from Tom rocking up head to toe with the most horrific sunburn I'd ever seen, and making my then months-old niece, Lacie scream at the very sight of him. But he made up for it in charm and politeness and my parents loved him. That meant the absolute world to me and still does; although it has been painful admitting that my Dad was right about all of my relationships.

We had the most amazing first few months together. We shared experiences that even now have us in hysterics, but to most, would probably seem a bit strange. We look back on our early dates with great fondness, even if they went so badly that most people would have called it a day. Our first date was spent by the side of the road, the second saw Tom throwing up and managing to kick me in the face as he did so, and our fourth was spent in A&E after Tom injured his foot at football. But we handled it all with humour and spent our time doing impersonations of gangster tractors, went on endless adventures together and even started to build our very own Ms Pacman arcade machine. After just 5 months I had moved in and everything was perfect; I don't think either of us thought it would come crashing down as abruptly as it did.

We had never really argued at this stage. If I was annoyed, I would go quiet, but Tom always knew how to fix things. Maybe it was the engineer in him, I don't know, but he always had a plan and could always make things feel like they were going to be okay. Out of the two of us, he was definitely calmer, in fact, it would annoy me how chilled out he could be at times. So, it was perhaps more of a shock that of the two of us, Tom was the one to end up so unwell and so out of control.

I still remember the first time I saw Tom lose control. In May 2013 we had been to an evening event hosted by Tom's work and by all accounts were having an amazing time. There had been a couple of niggles through the night but nothing significant, and afterwards we had gone to a small local pub with a few of his workmates. We were all pretty drunk by this point and I had said something to Tom- it was so trivial that neither of us can remember now what it was, but with that, he walked out of the pub. At first, I thought he had gone to the toilet or to call a taxi, but when he didn't return, myself and his friend followed and found him; lying face down on the floor under a nearby arch, repeatedly plunging his fists into the concrete. For the first of many times, worrying for his physical safety, I positioned my hand between his and the concrete to try and stop him from injuring himself.

In what I genuinely believe was an effort to stop me
from getting hurt, Tom pushed me away, causing me to fall into a wall. He didn't even realise that this had happened and just sobbed uncontrollably. With that, a police van pulled up and me and his friend proceeded to try and explain to the officer that he was just drunk and emotional and wasn't a risk to anyone, properly scared that he would get arrested. Luckily the officer knew Tom from school and knew that this was out of character, so he drove us back to Tom's friend's house where we spent the rest of the night trying to calm him down and get hold of his dad to pick us up. Tom calmed down, and we cleaned his hands up and I don't think we actually told his dad what had happened.

When we got home, things went from bad to worse. I was angry, embarrassed and also extremely confused as to where that had come from. I tried desperately to get Tom to explain to me what was going on, but he couldn't; he didn't know, and the more I pushed, the more distressed he became. He became more and more angry and before we knew it had ripped shelves down in one of the bedrooms, punched doors and thrown everything in his reach. I had no idea what to do other than beg him to stop, which eventually he did, and we spent the rest of the night holding each other.

The devastation we felt the next morning when we both woke up and stone-cold-sober had to look at the destruction left behind. It almost hurt more than seeing it first-hand the night before.

Over the following months, this became an all too familiar routine. On the surface, we still looked like the perfect couple. We carried on going to work, having nights out and plastering our love for each other all over social media as if nothing was happening. But behind closed doors, I didn't recognise the man I was living with. It's hard for me to admit this, because most of my jobs have been in Mental Health, and I'm trained to understand and manage all the things that Tom was going through, but I was so angry that I forgot about all of that.

I was angry that our house was destroyed, angry that I was having to take so many days off work or miss nights out with friends because I was having to spend such a vast amount of time trying to manage his outbursts.

I was angry that I felt so responsible for cleaning up the mess and destruction left behind and above all, I was angry that through all that, Tom wasn't even able to give me an explanation. In fact, most of the time, he would blame me. *"You pushed me too far"*, *"it's your fault, you wouldn't leave me alone"*, and *"there's nothing wrong with me"* became almost an anthem for the next couple of years. In part, looking back, I agree.

There were times when the professional in me wanted to fix Tom, and I guess I thought that if I kept asking, eventually he would give me the answers I was looking for and then I could help. But also, I know now that often when Tom would go into what we've since referred to as "hulk mode", he was actually in Psychosis and had very little recollection or insight into what was happening. To him, his actions were perfectly justifiable and were the result of a problem with the world around him and definitely not with himself.

I look back on some of these early events and I am filled with deep regret that I let my own anger get in the way of supporting Tom in the way that he needed.

I know that it wasn't all my fault and maybe it wouldn't have made a difference, but I will always carry with me a niggling feeling that I could have done more at the beginning to stop things from escalating.
It all happened so quickly though. We were completely blindsided. Even now looking back, it's hard to believe it all happened because it feels like such a blur and some of it felt really bizarre.

Tom mentioned before that he once smashed his DJ decks over his head. It sounds bad enough as it actually was but honestly, I thought it was going to be so much worse. I got home from work like any other day and entered the dining room to see a trail of blood all over the floor and door handles. It was just like a movie in which I had to follow the trail of blood to find Tom. At that point, I was preparing myself to find a body. It sounds extreme but there was so much blood, I really didn't expect to see him sitting in the living room, extremely calm, just trying to stop the bleeding. It was a shock but also a relief that he was alive.

I remember other things around this time that I still don't fully understand. Sometimes, if he'd had a particularly bad day, I would get home and find Tom sat on the living room floor having hacked chunks out of his hair. He would just be staring at the pile on the floor. Ironically, he was so depressed at this point, he was neglecting his personal appearance massively, so this was the only time he'd ever actually have a haircut.

This was such a small, strange thing to happen, but had such a huge impact on Tom's confidence. He was no longer able to keep up the façade to the public that everything was okay. The evidence was hacked into his hair for all to see. So, he started to stay indoors more, and if he did venture out, he would wear a hat or keep his hood up as if he was trying to make himself invisible to the world. This in itself made his mental health get so much worse, and our relationship become so much more fraught, because not only were Tom's outbursts happening on almost a weekly basis but as I was only working part-time, we were now constantly under each other's feet.

I have to admit, I wasn't really coping at this point. I couldn't talk to Tom about how it was all affecting me because it would invariably lead to an argument and I was very aware that I didn't want to make him feel worse than he already did. He was so consumed by everything that whenever I did open up to him, he appeared to feel persecuted and like he was being cornered, so it only ever served to make his symptoms worse. I did confide in a few friends, but the reactions I got at the time were often sympathy for me and a judgement that Tom's behaviour was out of order and a reason for me to leave him.

This wasn't what I wanted. I desperately needed someone to speak to and did consider confiding in my parents for support. However, they loved him, and mental health has such an awful stigma attached to it that I had no idea how they would react. I didn't want them to see Tom any differently. Mental illness is one of those things that only seems to be talked about by people living through it, so it was never something I'd talked about with anyone around me.

This is something that is incredibly important to me now. If mental health was talked about more in general conversation, I would have felt much more comfortable talking about it when I needed to. I often think that perhaps if that had been the case, I could have had more supportive outlets for my feelings and then would have felt more able to help Tom. Perhaps things wouldn't have escalated as much as they did, who knows?

My advice to everyone reading this, whether you have experience with mental illness or not, is to make it a normal topic to talk about, just like any other illness. It normalizes it and lets those who are suffering know that you're a safe person to approach if they ever need support.

I see a lot of Facebook posts nowadays with people stating: "*my kettle is always on, it's okay to talk to me about mental health*", and they make me so happy. You have no idea how valuable these are to people who are desperately searching for someone to open up to. I'm confident that they will have a huge impact on preventing more people from having a similar story to ours. For me, if I'd seen things like that when we needed support, our story may have stopped here, things may have been easier.

Chapter 7 – Who said that? (T)

Anxiety – *The feeling of constant worry or fear which can range from being mild to absolutely soul destroying.*

My life was now about to take a further nosedive. Anxiety was now starting to get the better of me. Simple things were now starting to get harder and harder, even just leaving the house to go to the shops made me feel like everyone was watching me and scrutinising my every action. This started to affect my work and I would start avoiding certain duties because of the pressure I put on myself and how I assumed no one liked me.

Naturally, this flowed down to affect my friends; killing my social life as by now they did not bother to ask if I was going to do things with them, I only saw them roughly one day a week at best and that was to play football when I would give out my best impression of being okay.

Amber didn't know either at this point. We were inseparable and yet I didn't tell her any of the issues I was experiencing. I really started to struggle to do anything, this included anything around the house and because of this Amber obviously started to get annoyed with me because I wasn't doing my bit.

It wasn't because I was lazy, it was because at the time what I was going through was completely debilitating, but for unknown reasons.

I would even go back on the games console and push her away unknowingly just to hide my own issues as some sort of safety blanket. See if I enter that online world as a different persona, I didn't have to deal with the reality and the gravitas of what I was going through.

Little did I know at this point that this was the opposite I should have done.

As soon as I came back from disassociating myself from playing the latest survival horror and "Re-entered" my own life; I immediately became a horror to be around. I would be snappy; I would have a short fuse, and arguments were becoming even more common. It was the only escape I knew; I didn't want to be me in reality so online I was playing a character by the name of "Sirsmudge".

My friends didn't really see eye to eye with Amber, in fact, they never really did. I didn't consider these people to be my friends but my family so I callously excused what they were saying and not protecting amber when she needed it; with my history, the last thing I wanted was for them to leave me. I thought at the time that these were the only thing stopping me going back to the way I was back in school, alone. I took the wrong side and pushed my love away further – and even still, it gets worse.

Amber would tell me in all honesty what they were saying behind my back to her, but I wouldn't believe it. Not because of anything Amber has done, but because I believed at this point, that my group of friends didn't have a single toxic bone in their bodies. Again, I was massively wrong.

Outside of the social circles, my anxieties would follow me. The place I worked is a large-scale factory where if I responded to a breakdown or a machine had a fault on it, it could take around 15 minutes just to get there walking. During 15 minutes after accepting the task; my brain would be occupied with hostile thoughts, not of what I should do, or how can I fix it; but more of *"What would people think of me if I couldn't fix this problem myself?"*; *"What would have happened if I broke it further?"* Or even *"Do they even like me?"*

At this very moment in time, I never really thought anything was wrong. I figured that this was just me and that it was just the very specific way I was wired up and how I was made to operate in life generally.

This would progress further –I think it all started on a night shift. I would be doing the usual trek from one part of the factory to another in response to a call from my site radio. Walking through a part of the factory, which was just a large empty warehouse, I heard someone say *"Oi, fat boy!"* I immediately was rooted to the ground like a tall oak maturing – it felt like decades had passed before I could move.

I managed to spin on the spot and look around only to find no one was there.

Now this voice was not an internal thought, like one where you contemplate what time that programme you wanted to watch starts; no, this was a voice, coherent as if being spoken to face to face with another being. As if the sound waves were reverberating across my eardrums "real."

This temporary paralysis eventually gave over and I was able to carry on with my task at work, and just shrugged it off, putting it down to me being stressed and tired.

I heard it again through the night with the identical outcomes but again I just shrugged it off – you could say, bottling it up as I did with my brothers passing.

Back at home, it would develop into something so much worse. Amber and I would have our own little arguments, no couple is perfect but this eventually became a daily occurrence – no fault of my better half. It would start with me hearing something completely out of context or even completely wrong and then I would start to hear this voice speaking all over again. With the argument unfolding in real life, this voice would then chime in. "*She hates you*" – it would state. This coherent voice would then be joined with a friend. "*She deserves better than you!*" the other manifestation would add, only this time it was like another person had entered the conflict.

Both of these voices were completely different; accents and tones I'd never heard before. It was just like two people had burst into my house and wanted to join in the argument.

This obviously overwhelmed me and this caused something catastrophic to take over.
Whatever it was which kept me in control, sane and collected was somehow pushed aside and something else had jumped into the driver's seat.
"*Throw that ornament!*" one of the voices would say.
"P*unch that door!*" the other would command.

I could do nothing but do as these "beings" commanded; smashing and slamming my way around the house.

Amber, of course, was in danger of being hit with any shrapnel or loose objects as they were hurled as makeshift projectiles across various rooms, but the commands, or thoughts, or whatever they were, never told me to hurt Amber. I never gave her any physical abuse or took my anger out on her but like I said, she may have been caught in the crossfire.

Once the chaos was starting to settle down, it really felt like whatever had its control on me, decided that it had had its fun and now it was time for me to pick up the pieces.

Slumped on the floor, mumbling to myself and bursting into fits of tears, Amber could do nothing but look on. She didn't dare come anywhere near me; I don't blame her to be honest. I didn't dare look myself in a mirror to see what I had become.

The day went and still, I couldn't tell Amber what had happened.

I mean she was there and fully aware of what happened on the outside, but on the inside where the real war was starting to unfold, I didn't really know what to say. I didn't even know what was going on – What if it's just how I am wired. How I was made and what I was supposed to do on the planet?

This went on for weeks on end; when the malevolent force took over my actions it started to turn self-destructive and take everything out on me. a common theme was that my fists would be swollen and bloodied; struggling to walk because I kicked a door frame or tried to put my foot through a brick wall – but the worst one was when Amber wasn't even there.

On the rare occasions when I was invited to play football, I could vent all my issues on the pitch when I was running around and put it down as passion for the game; but there was one night where all of a sudden, last minute, they all cancelled on me. I don't know to this day what really happened but I'm putting it down to the borderline personality disorder (Which at this time, I had no idea was a thing).

The irrational voice would say *"That's it, they don't want you now."*

I grabbed the nearest thing to me at the time which unfortunately was my DJ decks. They were sat on the dining room table after their previous use, and I repeatedly smashed this into my skull. Amber was on her way home from work at this point and thought that I was out with friends.

I found out that the scalp has hundreds of capillaries in it and once you've cut one or more, blood seemed to rain down like I was playing "Carrie" in the end of the movie with the same name (Sorry, spoiler alert.)

I remember the blood cascading down all sides of my head making it feel that there was a thick liquid showering me from somewhere ethereal.

I threw the now destroyed DJ equipment to the floor; touched my head with both hands and then to my horror saw my hands thickly covered in the viscous liquid which definitely shouldn't be outside of my circulatory system.

I started to panic.

My head felt like it was in the clouds.

I ripped the football shirt off my body and held it to my head begging for this to stop.

My full attention had gone from acknowledging these beings and delusions to now being grounded and in the moment.

Amber walked in. Perfect timing.

Amber walked in on me, drenched in blood with my football top pressed against my head in an attempt to not drain my body like a carcass in an abattoir.

All credit to her though, she kept her cool and checked if I was okay, then called an ambulance. This would be the rare occasion where I wouldn't end up being put in the back of the wagon and sent to A&E, little did I know that this would get even worse.

Amber said for the first time. *"Do you want me to call your Dad?"* *"No!"* I would snap back. My dad now lived a good hour away and the last thing I wanted to do was pull him away to take care of me.

My father during his time in the RAF had been to various warzones and conflicts all over the world, my problems are in no comparison to what he had seen and been through – in all honesty, I was half expecting him to tell me *"Man up"* or *"What have you got to be upset about?"*

Even with all of this going on, I still didn't see anything wrong with me. I thought I was fine; nothing was ultimately wrong and that it was just who I was. Every time this happened, I broke down and cried to myself, it was few and far between that Amber would see me in tears. History had proven to me that if I were to break down and cry that I would get bullied, tormented and even isolated; the fact that I had someone who cared for me and had a set of friends who seemed to like me for me, there was no chance that I was going to risk going back to that.

Chapter 8 – The voices are talking to me (A)

I think this is the point where the fear set in. I had seen Tom's outbursts deteriorate from smashing things up to him experiencing hallucinations, too serious self-harm and then all of a sudden, ambulances were being called most weeks. Things were definitely out of control and I had long since stopped knowing what to do.

I know a huge concern from Tom when he was lucid was that he never wanted me to be scared of him. At 6 foot 4 inches, it would be fair to assume that these outbursts were quite intimidating to witness. But the truth is, I was never scared of Tom.

I don't know why, and many would probably think I was stupid, but I just knew deep down that he didn't want to hurt me. Sometimes Tom would let me know what the voices were saying to him and without exception, they were always wishing harm towards him and telling him to destroy things around him.

They would tell him that I was better off without him, and I learnt very quickly that whatever was driving these voices seemed to have some strange kind of empathy for me. It was like in Tom's mind, it was them and me against him. There were times where I could use this to our advantage and as strange as it sounds, I would have entire conversations with the voices, with Tom acting as a conduit for us to communicate.

I was able to almost manipulate them by telling them that by hurting Tom they were hurting me, and for a while, they would disappear. However, a respite from them was short-lived, and as quickly as they'd go, they'd be back with a vengeance, doing anything they could to hurt him. This is what I was afraid of. Nothing I could do for Tom was having any real impact. I could keep him safe for a short while but knew that he was extremely volatile and wouldn't be safe for long.

I knew I needed someone else to help us. The only person I could think of who lived anywhere near us was his dad. I knew that he would support Tom no matter what but was terrified that he would somehow think this was all my fault, after all, this only started after we met. At this point that didn't matter. I was willing to be hated by everyone, to sacrifice our relationship if that meant that Tom would be ok. I knew that the need to help him was bigger than me and all my selfish worries. I have never been so nervous as the day I first picked up the phone and called Lea. It was gone midnight and after hours of Tom smashing everything in sight, punching himself and anything he thought may hurt enough, I couldn't manage it anymore.

I picked up the phone and dialled for an ambulance and as soon as I hung up, called his Dad. I woke him up, and in an effort to not worry him too much, told him that Tom had been struggling for a while and was having a breakdown and asked him to meet us at A&E.

I knew Tom would be mad and feel betrayed and embarrassed, but I didn't care. Seeing Lea walk into the A&E waiting room that night, I felt instantly calm. For me, and I think for Tom as well, knowing that we now had his support was a huge weight lifted. It was embarrassing feeling like we were airing our dirty laundry a little, but it meant that Tom had someone who wasn't me to turn to, and this helped us both to some extent. He was, however, still extremely poorly. Every trip to A&E resulted in the same thing: a physical check by often lovely triage nurses, followed by a four-hour wait to see the overstretched Crisis team, a brief chat which always ended in Tom lying that he could keep himself safe to be allowed home, and then nothing... until the next time.

Every second I was away from Tom, I was terrified of what was happening. If he didn't text back within a few hours, I was convinced he was dead. I was waiting for that dreaded phone call from the police or hospital to tell me he'd killed himself. I would have preferred him to be taking it out on me than himself because at least then I would know he was alright. There were times when he would text me at work and I knew he wasn't right.

He would text me and tell me the voices were back, or he would tell me about what he was going to do to harm himself. Other times, his messages would make little sense, and any attempt by me to get more information from him would just make him angry, because to Tom, he was making perfect sense and I was the one talking nonsense. Sometimes I was able to get home to him, but others, there was no way I could get there. I cannot describe the fear I felt. The anxiety, knowing that the person I loved was so close to the edge, and that I was too far away to help.

I remember once having a call from Tom at around 8 am whilst I was on my way to Boston for work with my amazing friend and colleague, Julie. I had no idea what he was saying but he was so distressed and was begging for help. I had no way to get to him because he was over 30 miles away from us. All I could do was try to calm him down using what Julie now fondly refers to as my "sexy voice". He eventually assured me that he was going to sit in his car and calm down and then go home. Later that day I had a call from one of his workmates trying to explain an incident that had happened, and that he was extremely worried about Tom. I felt so guilty that I'd hung up, convinced he would be ok, and now, he wasn't picking up the phone. All I could think was that the worst had happened.

I felt so humbled at this point by the team I was working with. I'd only known some of them for a couple of months and between them, they figured out that a taxi would cost me around £40 to get home and they rallied around to scrape together enough to lend me as I was completely broke. (Something, we rarely consider on the journey of mental illness is that it's bloody expensive.) With every hospital trip came a taxi home which combined with replacing doors and various broken bits meant I never had any money to spare.

Thankfully, somewhere amongst all this, Tom had managed to contact his dad and I later found out he'd made it home, spoken to the Crisis Team, and his dad had calmed him down enough to be safe until I arrived home. I really don't know how I would have coped without so many people looking out for us. Julie alone was a huge support for me. We both worked in mental health roles and I knew she understood and wouldn't judge. She is also one of the funniest people I know and kept me distracted, knowing exactly how to cheer me up.

I am so thankful for everyone who tried to help us, especially her. I learnt that having a support network was vital for us both. The only way we would survive this would be if we had people separate from each other to turn to. Even though things were horrific at home, and if anything, were getting worse, I knew there was help there and on the darkest days, that kept me going.

My only regret was that I didn't realise this sooner. Fear of judgement and shame that I couldn't fix this all myself stopped me from asking for help and that in turn meant that neither Tom nor I ever stood a chance of things getting better in those early days.

Chapter 9 – The conflict between reality (T)

This lack of control started to become more frequent. First of all, it was weekly with a two-day clean-up of all the fall-out; then it started to become daily.

Amber would do her best every time to try and control this, but she could only see the destruction in her path while she tried to hold me back not for her protection, but for my own. I was throwing things left, right and centre and now, for the first time – I was completely gone. For the whole two years this kept going on and getting worse, I could not see what was going on, it wouldn't save in my memory, my mind would be vacant like a freshly formatted memory stick.

There was an odd anomaly to this though. As if it couldn't get any worse with me losing control; I was now challenging the very fabric of reality – But this wasn't when I was in psychosis.

The voices were getting stronger and starting to affect my actual thought patterns. Getting more and more deluded thoughts which just fuelled the psychotic rages into something more comparable to Bruce banner turning into The Hulk.

One night which I want to be removed from my memory; while the nightly chaos unfolded before Amber's eyes, I had a visitor. I was in the dining room with Amber screaming at me, pleading for me to stop.

A familiar stranger had broken into my house, "*How did HE get in*" I questioned.

Will, my brother would all of a sudden be in the room, just stand there.

No expression, dressed in the same clothes as when I said goodbye in the chapel of rest seven years before, silently judging me; judging everything while the chaos unfolded.

Every room I escaped to; Will would be standing there; waiting. I did my best to get away from Amber, who as you could imagine was petrified, trying to keep her safe from the crossfire.

Will would be stood; with the same blank facial relaxed expression; the exact expression he had on his face in the chapel of rest, except this time his eyes were wide open –following me around the room like the horror movie trope of a painting following their prey with their eyes. After this, I don't remember anything. I had fully lost control. My brain pulled the plug on my memory and I have no recollection of what happened in the meantime.

I "woke up"; regained control, became sane - whatever it was, I came around in a packed A&E with my head resting on the shoulder of my love; a very exhausted and red-eyed Amber.

"*How did I get here and why was I in A&E when there was nothing wrong with me?!*"

My hero Amber told me everything that had happened and I listened in horror Not for what I had done to myself or the position I was in (I didn't care about that) I was mortified of what I put her through.

I can't imagine what it must have been like for her, knowing full well that she did her best, but for no

positive outcome; also having to see her 6ft 4"
boyfriend completely lose control of his actions and of
the very fabric of reality.

After beginning to regain an ounce of control
and being aware of my surroundings I started to quiz
Amber to make sure she wasn't physically harmed by
me or my actions – Thankfully, she wasn't but was
obviously shaken by what had happened.

It was the early hours of the morning, and I
figured that it was just me and Amber, I didn't want
anyone to know what was going on because selfishly,
I didn't want anyone to think I was beating my partner
and causing a torrent of emotional and physical
domestic abuse; nor the fact that I was in a significant
amount of distress and was very unwell.

My Dad entered A&E.

I thought I was starting to lose my mind again.
*"Amber wouldn't have called him, surely? she knows I
really didn't want him to know; so how could he have
known I was here?"* It didn't make any sense to me,
but of course the reality being, Amber had called for
help.

He glanced across with a smile on his face and
took the spare seat next to me while Amber was on the
other shoulder. He turned to me and asked the question
which like so many before, will stay with me forever -
"Are you okay? Amber called me."

No emotions were being registered at this
point, my head was spinning and it seemed that it
couldn't comprehend any emotion at all.

I was numb.

No embarrassment.

No shame.

No sadness.

My brain had officially shutdown from external stimuli and entered a sort of "Safe mode" to protect not just the fingertip grip on reality, but to protect my overall psychology in general.

A common theme through my life as I'm sure you have already realised; is that there are snippets of dialogue which have etched themselves into my memory and this next one is no different.

Dad asked in the most concerned, calm and loving voice "*Why didn't you tell me?*"

"*...I don't know.*" I murmured back as tears started to make their pilgrimage down the side of my face.

This may seem like I was lying again but in truth, I wasn't.

If you think about it, I really had no idea why I didn't tell him. It's easy saying that now because obviously, I know of mental health and the effects it has on someone, but this idea of "Man up" which I felt when Will had died is nothing but hot air and actually quite pathetic.

What is "Manning up?" Holding all your problems in and showing the world that you're an emotionless husk, drifting through life living in a permanent state of contempt; or is it opening up when you have a problem and tackling the problem head-on? Thankfully, somehow this exact sentiment is now starting to enter my mind, like an acorn waiting to sprout into a tall oak.

Sat in A&E with the love of my life holding my arm, cuddled up to my shoulder while my dad and I essentially talked about nothing but football scores and our beloved Rochdale AFC, while we waited for our turn with the Crisis team.

I had no idea they existed at this point and no idea of their support function. We were shown into a meeting room and then entered the crisis support worker.

She must have known that I was really struggling and so made an unexpected joke. I found that to be a great icebreaker and that it helped ground me further. My brain needed to be kickstarted into some form of cognitive entity and she did just that.

I listed my problems and FINALLY, it felt like the weight of the world had lifted from my shoulders. I wasn't really given any more help during this session except I was now equipped with the crisis teams contact details should we ever need them in the future. Dad gave us a lift home, dropped us off and then we went straight to bed. This whole scenario became as often as every few days; it even became predictable.

Outside of the home, work was now getting unbearable. I was putting on this massive façade of there being nothing wrong and that I was ready for everything, but it was starting to crack.

I would sneak off at work and lock myself in the toilets away from anyone, so they couldn't see how this front was starting to fragment into nothing. The twenty-minute drive to and from work was starting to get dangerous.

The number of times where I just wanted to turn my car off the main carriageway and straight into the concrete wall of the overpass bridge was increasing and was starting to get more and more appealing.

After a particularly stressful day, I could feel the weight of my actions over what I had forced Amber to go through; the worry I'd caused my dad, and the desolate feeling of "Is this just me?". The intrusive, deluded thought that there is no help available, which would help get me through this made me want to stop it there and then.

The elusive bridge was approaching in the distance and my foot hit the floor.

60 mph, 70mph, 80mph (it was only a small car so it wouldn't go any faster) and I started to straighten the car up on the bend of which the foot of the bridge was home to.

Within a split second, I started to slow the car down and continued my journey down the dual carriageway back home.

In between the thought of certain suicide and then wanting to remain on this world, I entered that reality which I once entered when trying to take that overdose back at school age.

I could think of no one but Amber. How much I loved her and then my family. To put it in some form of comparison, it was like seeing your life flash right in front of you and all the reasons why you are even on this planet to begin with.

To this day, I have no clue what happened. Time stood still while 20+ years of memories flooded in.

I remember feeling like I was stood in a bright open room staring at a huge projector screen.

The day me and Amber met.

The Airband in the latter parts of my school years.

Josh and Michael.

My entire family.

I came back just at the right moment and had to make a do-or-die movement as my car edged across the rumble strip to avoid a collision. I got back on the road, in my own lane and proceeded to drive home. I was exhausted. I just wanted to be home.

This thought definitely wasn't mine but it definitely saved my life. I got home, but I couldn't tell Amber any of this. She was already worried about what was happening at home, she didn't need reasons to be worried about me simply going to work.

A few days elapsed and I was back in the factory on the normal inspection routines, I found myself on a platform which was easily about 10 or 12 stories high. My first thoughts were in awe of the view, I like being high up and seeing the world from a new perspective, but this was immediately poisoned with the echoes of a few days before on THAT journey home.

"That would definitely do it." Something exclaimed.

I didn't think this. This was a voice. What was happening to me?

"You don't have to do a thing" someone else suggested

"Do it!" I was commanded.

I looked around to maintain a grasp on my already slipping psyche to see no one around me at all. I fell to the floor clasping the handrails in pure desperation.

"You're pathetic; you know that right?" A voice reminded me.

I wanted to flee this situation but, how could I? wherever I went these things followed me; and that's when I remembered The Crisis Team.

I took out my phone and with a death grip so as not to drop it, as if it was my final lifeline for survival; I dialled the crisis team.

I felt encircled by bullies like back in school. I panic dialled the crisis team, begging for someone to pick up. With the calm tones of "*Hello*" The voices stopped. Beautiful, sweet silence from this imperious torment. I broke down into a quivering mess, grabbed the handrail and was totally inconsolable. After about an hour I came back to my senses and just wanted to get my shift over and done with.

There wasn't really a great deal of work they could do over the phone, but they could help ground me again. Grounding is a technique which helps the psyche realise what is real and what isn't; to be fair it's quite the lifesaver.

They explained over the phone that an ambulance was on its way, I was pleading them to cancel it. I was at work and the last thing I needed right now was people to think I was dangerously insane. If it was a physical injury that's different, but the thought of having the workforce watching me enter an ambulance when there weren't any signs of injury made me feel incredibly degraded.

"*What kind of counsellor would I be if I didn't call you an ambulance after everything you've said?*" They replied back, justifying the reasons for their actions.

This was a very good point. They didn't really have a choice; I would have done the same. At the time I absolutely hated the person I was talking to; I broke down into tears shouting to the Team Leader over the inter-work radios.

"*Can you call me please...*" I muttered, holding back any evidence of my issues.

"*Sure...*" the team leader replied.

With the Crisis Team on my mobile in one hand, my work phone went off in the other. I relayed everything which was going on and to my surprise, much like my Dad, he was very open and welcoming.

I told the Crisis team that I was in the reception and in the company of my team leader; we agreed to end the call safe in the knowledge that help was on the way and I was in safe company.

My team leader was inquisitive as to what was going on and he kept saying that he was sorry for not knowing more or even what he should be doing in a situation like this. Not for one moment did I blame him for this, *I* didn't even know what was going on or what *I* should be doing, never mind what he should be doing! How was he going to know?! In the half an hour between telling him what was going on and the ambulance turning up; I did nothing but cry on his shoulder as I tried to explain the turmoil that my brain seemed hell-bent on sending my way.

The ambulance arrived and off to the hospital I went. When I got there the same routine was followed; asking if I was okay, what I wanted from them to help me which I STILL had no idea and that if I needed any more medications. After that, I set off home back to the comfort of Amber.

Circa 1996
Back: Rob (Brother, Left) and Will (Brother, Right)
Front: Deborah (Mum, Left) Tom (Centre) and Lea (Dad,
Right)

2002 – Tom starting Secondary School

2006, Tom and Billy in GCSE science – Listening to The Who – "Baba O'Riley"

2012, when we were happy and where our journey begins

Company end of season ball. Hours before the first episode of psychosis.

Amber and Tom on first holiday abroad; Two days after psychosis at best friend's birthday party

Emotional and exhausted, Tom and Amber putting on a brave face to family, letting their niece play makeup; after a long night in A&E

Henry and Luna

Where Amber said Yes!
Verona 2015

The happiest day of our lives.
12th March 2017

Tom with Lucas and his football team.

Tom sharing a beer with Lucas, One year to the day of his Cardiac Arrest

Tom and Josh, 24 years on and still close friends

Top – 2019 (28 Years old)
Bottom – 1995 (4 Years old)

Amber at the "Let's Talk Mental Health" Conference

Tom hosting TEDx Youth @Brayfordpool 2019

Amber and Tom at the
Active Lincolnshire Awards
2019

Chapter 10 – "It's a long road out to recovery from here." (T)

The next day I returned to work and treated it if it was a new day, and nothing had happened. The only issue now was, I was fully aware that everyone knew about what I was going through.

Everywhere I went I felt like everyone was looking at me. Judging what I was going through; the worse thing is I was in the belief that people were going to be talking behind my back. Paranoia had its claws firmly embedded in me; with it being so far rooted I couldn't escape it.

The 20-minute drive to work felt like four hours.

Anxiety, Paranoia and Depression; not the best combination in the world might I add.
I went in knowing I had to be strong. The day went by like any other, except I could just feel something wasn't right.

Not in my head this time, but with those around me; every time I walked into a room the conversation just stopped which to anyone would surely cause alarm bells to ring.

My paranoia was confirmed. Most of that day I spent sitting in the toilet; hiding my very existence. I made myself believe I was a troll which was hidden away and didn't want to come out because I was different.

Little did I know that this was the least of my concerns.

I got home and as if by clockwork, Amber and I would start to argue about things that were so little and that would be it.

"*She hates you.*" One voice would say.

"*You deserve no one*" another would add.

You know, the usual situation. Except this time was different; Amber had her bags packed and was now going to walk out of my life. The house was in pieces yet again, my hands were bloodied and swollen to the point I barely had any movement in them and the sound that haunts me to this day – the door slamming shut.

I sprinted out and screamed, "*Don't leave me!*"

Amber had finally had enough.

I don't blame her really, I put her through incredible amounts of emotional distress and pain. She did everything she could and this was the last straw, she needed to focus on herself for once.

I don't blame her one bit.

She was half out the front gate when I painfully grabbed her by the arm.

I dropped to my knees.

"*Please, please I need you*" I begged her. She said she just couldn't do this anymore and she can't see me do this to the house and to myself. Again, I don't blame her.

I carried on begging to her saying "*I'll get better, I'll change.*" with my face, bright red with emotion and sodden with tears. She finally turned to me and said "*Okay I'll stay, but you need to see someone. Agreed?*"

I could do nothing but agree and comply to the laid-out agreement.

The lifeline was thrown out to the murky quagmire of mental illness, I NEEDED to grab on for dear life.

I need to grab on for recovery.

I need to grab on for the love of my life.

That night we simply lay in each other's arms waiting for the new day to begin. The turning point out of this abyss.

I couldn't know at this point how much of a significance this next part would play out in the survival of the war against myself.

The morning came around just like any other. I got up, did my daily routine of breakfast, a cup of tea and a bit of TV, but the routine stopped as the TV came on. "*I better get this over and done with,*" I thought to myself, cocksure that the doctor would just turn me away and say there was nothing wrong.

Even though I had made this "Gentleman's' agreement" with Amber, I was fully expecting the doctor to not take it seriously. I was expecting a "*See me in two weeks when we can fit you in*" proving how little importance it was.

"*Can you come in the next hour?*" The receptionist asked, after hearing what my problems were.

"*Uh, yeah sure…*" I responded.

I was completely dumbfounded, perplexed even.

"*Nah nothing wrong with me*" I still foolishly reminded myself.

The hour went by and I walked into the doctor's surgery, signed in and waited for my turn.

My mood at this point was pensive at best. I had no idea what was about to happen, there is nothing wrong with me so why is there an air of suspense hanging over me like a low cloud, blanking my already blurry vision?

I must have been waiting no longer than two minutes when my name was called out. I could feel the glare of everyone around land on me like I had just walked in with nothing on but my underwear. The walk felt like a lifetime. *"why does something not feel right?"* I thought to myself.

I couldn't put my finger on it but I continued into the doctor's office. I tentatively sat down and essentially told him everything that happened. Within minutes of sitting in that chair and listing the horrors of what I put my loved ones through, he printed a small piece of paper. Scrawled over it in what can only be likened to a special doctor's code like the Egyptians and the hieroglyphics.

The page started with the words "Fit Note," I knew it! I was fine! I thought to myself as I let out a sigh of relief. My eyes glanced further down the paper.

• ***Reasons for Fit Note: Not Fit for work, Depression.***

The doctor went on to tell me that what I was going through was perfectly normal, but it was a genuine illness I had. I couldn't comprehend the fact that I was mentally unwell; I never thought mental health was even a thing.

He passed me another piece of paper which was the medication I required, Citalopram; a common anti-depressant.

I had encountered depression with people before, but I was always in the same mindset of *"Man up"* and *"There is nothing wrong with you."* – This is something which still haunts me and I can only help but think jokingly, that this was some twisted fate which the world bestowed on me for that very reason. He told me that I was on the waiting list for therapy with the CMHT (Community Mental Health Team) and that they will be in touch in the next few days to triage me. I thanked the doctor and walked out of the office.

I sat in my car, closed the door and the waterworks started. Although he said it wasn't, I couldn't help but think this was a death sentence.
"I'm insane, aren't I?" I kept asking myself.
"I'm beyond help!"
"I need to be locked up!"

I could only sit holding myself, rocking backwards and forwards. Lord only knows what someone would have thought if they saw me through the car window.

Once I calmed down, I phoned my next line of support; One which would be my constant, my rock and my foundation through this entire ordeal. I called Amber.

Amber told me to come home calmly and then we would talk about it. As soon as I got home, she had already gone and got loads of information on clinical depression, what its causes can be, statistics of suffering from the condition and an invaluable resource which I had never heard of before – TED talks.

If you haven't heard of these before, they are up to twenty-minute segments of a public speaker talking on anything from space, mental health or even business. I didn't know how valuable these would be going forward.

That day and most of the continuing night we watched hundreds of these talks from people who have suffered from various mental health issues and diagnosis and what they did to cope.

The next day I was supposed to turn up for my next shift at work, but now I had to phone them up and tell them that I was signed off work.

I took a deep breath and called my manager. My mindset was still that people were talking about me. Talking about the ambulance. Talking about how dangerous I was.

It was one of the hardest things I have ever had to do, to tell someone that I essentially couldn't work because of something going on in my head which in all honesty I didn't even understand. Thankfully they were very forthcoming and requested I sent them the doctors note.

I made this my next job, to get to the post office. I got this done and escaped back to the safety of my residence.

The subsequent days were merely a blur. I didn't really do anything except play my games console, waiting for Amber to come home like a dog waiting for its master to return; when I would feel I had relative safety from myself again. That was until my phone eventually lit up "Unknown Number."

My heart sunk. I remember looking at the screen and thinking to myself *"That's it, they are going to lock me up."*

It was the CMHT wanting to triage me. I wasn't really open to telling them anything; mostly for the fear of being sectioned or even locked up in an institution similar to what is usually portrayed in the media.

I eventually opened up and confessed to everything that was going on and they wanted to get me through to see the psychiatrist as soon as they could, but they warned me that it could be a *"considerable amount of time."* Oh, how right they were.

It would be around six or seven months until I was seen by the CMHT properly, but in this time my psychosis grew worse to again happening nearly every day.

One night, for example, Amber and I were coming back from the cinema after our date night, it was nice to just get out of the house.

I felt something wrong in myself and I could hear these insulting words being fired at me again from the very same voices as before. I was driving down a road on the way home as normal, Amber was sat beside me smiling because of the nice evening but little did she know what was going on in my consciousness.

I pulled the car over safely and hit the hazard lights.

As I reached out to hug Amber, I could feel the wave of emotion about to burst from me but that's when I noticed my hands were red.

Not just red from the lights of the dashboard, they were red with oozing blood.

I could see it clear as day, viscous congealing blood all over my hands as if I had just disembowelled something with my bare hands.

It came with a new sensory trigger, I could now smell it as well.

I started to panic, the voices started to laugh and even when I closed my eyes there was no escape. I was in that circle of bullies again.

Tormented, my hands covered in "blood", I became completely detached from reality. Thinking I was bleeding from somewhere and having no recollection of what was real and what was not, I blacked out. My autopilot came on as my brain had decided to protect me from the evil that had its talons firmly embedded – exactly like when I smashed the house up.

The next thing I know, I'm sat in A&E. I opened my eyes and found myself slumped against my only protection with her hand slowly tickling my head to try and ground and calm me. I looked down at my hands and could still see the blood. I couldn't smell it, but it was still there.

"What happened?" *"Is this mine?"* I questioned to myself.

I clung onto Amber like a lost child on their teddy bear; I needed guidance to find myself again.

I met the crisis team again where the same conversation of *"What do you want us to do about it?"* came up.

I hated this question. The more it was asked it made me wonder if they even cared. If I knew how to fix it and what would help, surely, I would have done that?

I was getting frustrated and the thoughts of not being unable to recover started to enter my head again. After a brief discussion, they promised to try and fast track my appointment with the CMHT psychiatrist and that would be the end of the conversation. We jumped into a taxi, got back to the car and then drove home – straight to.

A few weeks went by and I finally got my appointment to see the psychiatrist.

I felt like I was entering a world where not many come back from. I was fully expecting that now I knew something was wrong; maybe they will see I am not safe to be in society. I took a deep breath and thought to myself, if I'm going to get out of this mess, I need to get in there and listen to everything being told.

With every step walking into the reception, I began to realise how Neil Armstrong and Buzz Aldrin might have felt taking their first steps on the lunar surface.

It was one small step for understanding, one giant leap for my recovery.

I walked into the reception, logged in my attendance and took my seat in the reception. Thoughts were racing through my mind:
"Am I sane?"
"What is happening to me?"
"Will I be let out after?"
"When will be the next time I see Amber?"

The psychiatrist called me through, *"Here we go"* I sighed to myself.

The whole session lasted about an hour and a half. The psychiatrist told me that she was certain that the anti-depressant that I was on was not for me and was not working, so she moved me onto Fluoxetine (Prozac) and then added something for when the anxiety attack kicked in: Propranolol (Beta-Blocker) and to see how I got on. I was to be booked back in within two weeks to see how the medications had helped.

Two weeks had gone by and I was starting to feel a difference. As with any anti-depressant, it took a long time for the brain chemistry to take its effect and start to positively change my moods, To help stabilise me in fact.

I was beginning to smile more. I had been able to leave the house with friends for the first time in months by pretending to be soldiers by going Air-softing at a local ground and even going on evenings out with my family of friends. I was starting to see some positives.

One thing still lingered though, When I was at home, the intrusive thoughts started to re-emerge so, unfortunately, Amber would usually only see the bad side of me. It was no fault of hers, I think it was the house and seeing the trail of destruction I commonly left behind just added to the stress.

Hindsight is a beautiful/disgusting thing. Looking back I can see I wasn't getting better. I alienated and pushed Amber away, like I had at the beginning.

I returned to the psychiatrist and was finally given a list of diagnoses. First of all, she said that I require an anti-psychotic to prevent the issues with continually hearing voices and intrusive thoughts. She gave me Chlorpromazine in the meantime.

We went onto the diagnoses. She believed that I was suffering from Bipolar Disorder, the evidence from the few years showed where it was almost cycling and I could predict when the problems were about to occur; but we discussed that I was suffering from Borderline Personality Disorder.

Borderline Personality Disorder traits are commonly that of pushing people away because you're scared of them abandoning you; it's also very much like it says on the tin, Borderline. My moods could change on a knife-edge. Everything that happened previously, much like my friends cancelling on me for football one evening pretty much rubber-stamped this diagnosis as a certainty.

The next one was Severe Anxiety Disorder. I struggled to leave the house and was always on edge. Everyday Amber was not by my side I was living in a state where I was just waiting for my head to turn against me.

I didn't dare leave the house on my own because I could feel that everyone knew what I had put Amber through and were judging me as "That guy who emotionally abuses his girlfriend." This alone, answered numerous questions, even my down to my behaviour at work.

The final diagnosis came in the form of PTSD or Post Traumatic Stress Disorder. Immediately I knew it, yes, I agree wholeheartedly that I was a sufferer. We surmised that everything from the bullying, the assaults and Will's death had affected me and how I hadn't dealt with the reality and gravitas of the situation.

And there it is, the three diagnoses which now follow me through life: **PTSD**, **Severe Anxiety Disorder** and **Borderline Personality Disorder**.
I make this sound like it was over a short amount of time, but from seeing the doctor and being signed off work, to getting the diagnosis, this took between seven and eight months with regular counselling in between.

Arguments were still unfolding and my moods were getting worse; this was a sign of the fluoxetine entering my body as it adapted to the change in medication.

Like I said previously, it took roughly two weeks for it to enter my body and to take effect, once it did, I could feel my mood change. It was just enough to keep myself in control when I started to hear and see things;

and then it was time to see the psychiatrist for another follow-up.

I bounded into her office, positive that the chlorpromazine was not working. I was in a good mood but still listed the various side effects I was getting and how I was keeping a grip on my own reality – but only just.

She suggested taking a medication which was not registered for this use – Quetiapine.

Quetiapine is another anti-psychotic medication which its most common side effects were weight gain and drowsiness.

This was perfect to help me sleep at night but because it wasn't licenced for this use, I had to fill in a form and sign my name to say I was happy with the possible re-percussions and that it may not even work or even make me worse. It was experimental but I was in no place to argue; I was desperate for normality and to be fixed – I would try anything.

Not just for me, for Amber.

Chapter 11 – Some calm before the storm (A)

Through everything that had happened, for what had been a year or so of feeling constantly on edge, I never stopped loving Tom. Occasionally we would have incredible days, or even whole weekends, where things were ok. We would go on holidays or out for meals, laugh uncontrollably and almost convince ourselves that things were normal. I think it was days like that which kept me going as long as I did. Eventually, however, they weren't enough. I was exhausted.

Tom still refused to fully admit that he wasn't well and I was sick of getting the blame whenever something bad happened. The worst thing was having no idea what was going on inside his head. He was so unpredictable and I had started to experience awful anxiety attacks. It all reached breaking point for me on a night when as usual, Tom had been destroying things, trying to hurt himself, and I was unable to stop him, I just felt so out of control. Following him up the stairs, I got halfway and felt my legs give out. I had no energy and I couldn't breathe. Everything went fuzzy and I was terrified. I felt like I was dying, my chest hurt, and I couldn't stop shaking. I was begging Tom to help me, but he didn't. He couldn't.

I now know that I was having a panic attack, one of many that I'd end up having over the years. Somehow, I managed to drag myself back onto my feet, knowing that right then, I didn't have the luxury of being able to crumble. I needed to be strong in order to keep Tom safe. So, exhausted, I literally pulled myself up the stairs to see what had happened to Tom. As I did, I saw blue lights. Pure relief overwhelmed me. Our neighbours had heard my cries for help and called the police.

I later found out that they thought Tom was hurting me, and though this wasn't the case, I was so glad they cared enough to call for help. The police calmed things down and spoke to Tom. Frustratingly, the male officer who spoke to me refused to accept that Tom hadn't laid a finger on me and made me show him every room that Tom had destroyed as well as my arms and neck to prove I had no grab marks. I know that if I really was being abused, I would have felt relieved that someone cared enough to check. However, the problem for me was that as soon as the officer was satisfied that I wasn't the victim of abuse, that was it, they left.

My support ended.

He was one of many professionals who came into our nightmare and only tried to pull Tom out. I know I can appear extremely capable and confident, and probably made it seem like I had my shit together, but I needed someone to see that I was struggling.

I needed someone to ask if I could cope because there was no way that I would have told them that I couldn't otherwise.

That night, there were no ambulances available for several hours and Tom had calmed down significantly, so the officers agreed to leave him at home but only if he called his Dad for support. They also made us agree that we would call the doctors the following day. Tom agreed because he wanted them to leave; I agreed because I knew the only alternative was Tom spending the night at the police station, and there was no way I was going to let that happen. The following morning came, and ashamed, Tom refused to call our GP and curled up in our bed, ignoring me completely.

I tried to call and book an appointment for him, explaining to the receptionist that the police had advised us to do so and even telling her some of the things that had been happening to try and make her realise how desperately he needed an appointment. "I'm sorry, you aren't down as the next of kin so we're unable to speak to you- can Mr Dunning speak to us directly?" I tried to explain again how unwell he was and that he wouldn't speak at all. "I'm really sorry, it's confidentiality...I can't help" she responded. That sentence hit me like a truck. It was like the last glimmer of hope was gone.

With no appointment booked, I felt let down and trapped. My last hope of forcing Tom into the help I could clearly see he needed, had been taken away. Feeling like there was nothing more I could do, something inside me changed. I had given up.

I couldn't keep doing this anymore, and it felt like nothing would change. Our relationship had hit rock bottom, and although there were times where we could still laugh and enjoy each other's company, I didn't recognise the person Tom had become. Every good day was overshadowed by the fear that tomorrow would be a bad one. I could never truly enjoy any time with Tom because my role now was to keep him safe and alive.

Not only had I stopped feeling like his partner,

but I had also stopped feeling human. I was just robotically going through the motion's day by day. There was always this constant elephant in the room that neither of us knew how to talk about; we were both hurting, we both loved each other, but with every smashed door and broken ornament, we'd grown further and further apart until we no longer knew how to be there for each other.

I didn't want to look at Tom, he was a painful reminder of everything that had happened, and I couldn't bear to be in the house anymore because it was disgusting. Everything was broken and it's hard to find time to do housework when you spend every other evening in A&E. It was too much. The next day, I packed my bags, and when Tom got home and it started again, I walked out.

Every step I took down our path, I was praying for Tom to run out and tell me that he was sorry and that he would get help. I didn't want to leave. I'd built my entire life around this man, neglected friends, moved away from everything to be with him and I loved him. When I heard Tom running towards me, begging me not to leave, I felt relieved. That wasn't enough though, I needed to know that if I stayed, things would change. I told him that I would stay, that I would stand by him and support him as much as he needed, but that he needed to see a doctor. Much to my amazement, he agreed. In hindsight, I don't know what I would have done if he hadn't. I don't think I'd have actually been able to follow through and leave him, so it's lucky really that I didn't get to that point.

The next morning came, and Tom called the doctor himself. He didn't want me to go in with him which made me feel anxious, but I knew he needed space to talk honestly, this was a huge step for him. I just hoped that he would tell the truth.

I was extremely proud of him and for the first time in ages, I think we both had some hope. Tom being signed off work was difficult and adjusting to a new routine was hard on us both, but we knew it was necessary.

Tom started to open up to me more than ever before. He told me about some of the dark thoughts he'd been having, it was the first time he'd told me about any thoughts to end his life. I know this was difficult for him.

Often people who are experiencing suicidal thoughts don't want to burden or scare others, so they keep them hidden. I would say the opposite for me was true.

As soon as Tom told me how he was feeling, I felt relieved. I'd always thought he did want to kill himself, and his denial of that made it scarier.

The worst thing about Tom's mental illness for me was the unpredictability, the not knowing. I was worried that Tom might act on these thoughts, of course, but like with anything, mental illness is much less frightening if you know what you're facing.

Knowing what his main issues were, I was able to start finding ways to help Tom. I also felt relieved that there was no longer an elephant in the room. Once he'd said the words out loud, I felt comforted that he was being honest, and I felt like he might at least tell me if he was planning to act on those thoughts and that

I might be given the chance to help.

I think this is an important part of our story for those who might be having similar suicidal thoughts. There's a good chance that your loved ones will have recognised you're struggling long before you've told them, and not knowing what's happening is scary. Often, people only want to help, they just don't know how or where to start, so trying to share some of that with them, although scary, can help in the long term to be able to move forward. I also didn't realise at the time, the importance of asking about suicide. Tom didn't feel he could tell me for a long time, and I never thought to ask. It wasn't the right time to ask when Tom was in crisis, and when he was calm, it was like we had an unspoken rule to not remind him of what had happened.

I know now how empowering that question can be to someone who is experiencing those thoughts. It gives them the opportunity to open up and makes it easier for them to tell you; it also lets them know that you understand that this can be a common feature of mental illness and you care enough to want to help.

Once Tom had shared with me what he was going through, we tried to do as much as possible to help his recovery. We got out of the house as often as we could, and it was around this time that we bought our first dog, Henry. It might seem stupid buying a dog at a time when our future was so uncertain, but he helped no end. Tom had company when he was home alone and walking him was such a great outlet.

Things felt ok for a while and seemed to settle. There were still days when things were difficult, but nights spent in A&E were slightly less frequent than they had been. It was definitely better than before.

Chapter 12 – A love struck Romeo (A)

Over time, Tom began to confide in friends and family more. It made me so happy to know that he was finally starting to talk more about his Mental Illness. For me, it meant that he was starting to accept it and also, there were more people around to share the load when he needed support. I still felt anxious that people would find it difficult to hear, or that they would blame me as I so often did myself. However, the extra support and the fact that it was no longer a big secret, meant that we could begin to rebuild our lives.

After a while, I started to feel like Tom, and I had managed to get back to having a proper relationship and things seemed to be going well. In 2015, I decided to surprise Tom with a trip to Verona in Italy. We had talked for ages about travelling more and it was about time we had something to look forward to.

The holiday itself was perfect. We walked for miles taking in the beautiful sites, we laughed, we drank, we ate far too much, and we created some amazing memories which I hoped would take away some of the painful ones from the previous months. Without me realising, it seems that Tom had the same idea.

When Tom proposed (if you could call it that, but I'll leave it to Tom to tell that story); I was incredibly happy. I was pretty sure that if we could survive the hell we'd been through already, then marriage and all that came with it would be a walk in the park. He was clearly nervous and had even gone to the length of asking my dad for his blessing. Although I'm not particularly traditional, I appreciated the effort.

We couldn't wait to tell everyone. Keeping it a secret until we returned home and could break the exciting news to our family first, felt like torture. We decided together that we couldn't possibly tell everyone important in person. So, we told our immediate family and then, in true modern fashion, put a post on Facebook to share the happy news with everyone else. That way, we thought, everyone would be equal, and everyone could become part of the celebrations together.

How wrong we were! After all the crap life had thrown at us, we couldn't even have a happy engagement. Most people were over the moon for us and were already starting to mentally plan the big day. Swept up in all the excitement, we started to plan our engagement party and regale our friends and family with the details of how it happened! We noticed, however, that several of Tom's closest friends had been completely silent. Not even so much as a "like" on Facebook or a text to say congratulations. This weighed heavily on Tom and was like a black cloud hanging over what should have been a particularly exciting occasion. Tom decided to text one of the groups to ask why they'd been so quiet, and the response he got was a huge blow.

"*Oh, we thought it was a joke…*"

Clearly, as we'd shared photos of the ring, they didn't mean a "*ha-ha, just kidding*" kind of joke. What they meant was that they felt our engagement was a joke and that none of them believed our relationship would last after everything that happened.

I was furious but I have always maintained to Tom how important it was to keep his friends close. So, swallowing my own anger, I encouraged him to talk it through with them. We found ourselves somehow justifying our engagement. The elation we had felt days before had completely disappeared, and instead, there we were trying to convince Tom's friends that our relationship was serious.

Chapter 13 – Give me a break... (T)

Armed with the newfound knowledge of my various diagnoses and feeling like I now had some level of insight into why these things were happening to me, I gained a little bit of confidence; not a huge amount but just enough that I could open up to my friends about what was going on.

My life at home saw me starting to feel better and even happier than before; and then Amber and I, for the first time in a year did something, we planned for our lives in the future.

For Christmas, she had bought us a trip to Verona. A fantastic little holiday where we would be staying in a hotel with exclusive access to Juliette's balcony; Yeah that Juliette from the tragic love story "Romeo and Juliette"; Unbeknown to Amber in my pocket was the engagement ring. I wanted to promise my soulmate that I would spend the rest of my life with her.

I kept this well-hidden– Definite brownie points if I proposed in Verona!

From Christmas until our holiday in Italy in April of the following year; I focused more on my CBT (Cognitive Behavioural Therapy) but no longer just for Amber, I wanted to do this for myself also. It's one thing doing it for another person but having that newfound self-respect helped me engage in it further. I was finally getting the mindset of "*I'm going to beat this*" instead of just laying on my back exposing the soft side of my body and waiting for life to thrust the knife straight into my stomach.

The therapy I was receiving was simply an hour a week with a therapist and we would discuss and learn techniques on how to control my emotions.

The Diagnosis of borderline personality disorder made it essential that I knew how to control the disorder, rather than letting it go too far and allowing the disorder to control me.

I got more comfortable in my condition, started to master the reigns of my mental illness. The months followed and then came the day when we were ready to fly off to Italy.

It was a short flight but my mind was racing – finally, it wasn't to be because of being "shouted" at or how I was feeling, but how am I going to do it? With everything I had put her through would she ever say "yes"?

I think I must have put 3 kilos of weight on during the short flight alone but in muscle on my calves, I didn't stop tapping or shuffling throughout the entire journey.

We landed, got our transfer to the hotel. We left our bags there and decided although it was late, to go for an adventure. I kept the ring nestled in my pocket.We walked around the well-lit, historical streets of Verona and simply talked. It was lovely being in an alien place but safe in the knowledge that no one would know us, no one knew who we were and therefore, no stress. Amber kept changing sides which meant I had to skilfully move the box the ring was stored in without her seeing.

We entered the locked compound of Juliette's balcony as we had access to it via the hotel. I grabbed Amber in tight and amongst all the panic I didn't know what to say. What came out was the least romantic thing I have ever said; and I still get teased on it to this day.

"*Uhhh, Do I have to*?"

"*Do what*?" Amber tentatively replied

I dropped to one knee and said the words

"*Will you marry me*?"

Amber must have been overcome with emotion, or just wondering "*What do I do here?!*" because she replied with "*Oh!*"

"*That's not the reply I wanted really...*" I replied with an awkward chuckle under my voice.

"*Yes!*" she elated!

Finally, we were engaged. I was engaged to the love of my life. That night when Amber had fallen asleep beside me and I was trying to figure out what on earth was going on, in the Italian TV show we had on. I started to think back to everything we had been through in the six years of being together. How I had been on the verge of suicide, where it was pure luck that I was even still here; and now I'm going to be married to my hero and for once, I couldn't wait for the future.

After the mini-break, we had the inevitability of returning home. I was anxious but my positive outlook was helping to get me back to reality and my life back home.

Soon as we were home, I straight away told my friends everything. Everything about me, my disorders and my engagement.

Now, on face value, I was surprised to see that they were very happy that I had opened up to them. They could see the same as Amber could: I was visibly unwell. I didn't look after myself. Things were starting to get better but it was a far cry from what it should be. My personal hygiene was ropey at best, I let my hair grow and my poor attempt at growing facial hair only just made me look worse.

When I mentioned the engagement, one of those friends laughed and said, "*We thought you were joking.*"

I ignored this as a sort of power play, to take the focus off of me and to make them feel better because my life was starting to get back on track and gain traction.

Chapter 14-Hurt (A)

It would be fair to say that through most of our early relationship, I'd had some issues with Tom's friends. I've always been quite an introverted person and several of them felt that I wasn't making an effort. No matter what I did, whether it was inviting them round for house parties or giving Tom money so that he could go out alone with them, I was always the bad guy. There were times when we would bump into them in a supermarket and they'd stand there whispering about me. I know that sounds like I was paranoid, but one of them did later admit this to me; and even then, she made it sound like it was my fault.

Some of his friends were actually ok, and although I'm sure they were well aware of what the others were saying, they at least treated me with a bit of respect when we saw them. When people did decide to be horrible however, it was like they had this ability to home in on the one thing that would destroy my confidence or make me feel guilty. I never told Tom this, but at the birthday party of one of his friends, where he later went on to experience a psychotic episode; I confided in the brother of this friend who knew Tom quite well. I'm not sure if it was the alcohol or just the sheer hatred that group had for me, but his response floored me. "*No one likes you. You're not good enough for Tom. We've all thought for ages he should leave you.*" And then pointing across the garden to an old friend that Tom was talking to: "*and it's obvious he likes her.*" Those words would play over and over in my head for months afterwards, and rather than being just a horrible thought, became something that I believed completely.

It became glaringly obvious that many of his friends blamed me for Tom's Mental Health issues. I was told by several of them over the years that we clearly shouldn't be together, and that Tom had changed. I could understand this-often I would blame myself too. I constantly questioned whether I should walk away to make Tom happy. Tom always assured me that this wasn't what he wanted, but their words rang in my ears like sirens. I felt so unwelcome and so uncomfortable, but I was acutely aware that the worst thing I could do was to slag of Tom's closest friends to him. So, I would bury the hurt and anxiety they caused me and hid it with a smile as best I could. I have no idea how I managed to do this for so long; I think part of it was my fear that if I said it out loud, all those things would become true; and from that, a sheer stubbornness not to have a failed engagement at the age of twenty-two.

Despite their clear dislike for me, Tom's friends seemed to support him, and that was enough for me. All I wanted was for him to be happy, and so the impact it had on me became irrelevant.

There was a part of me that felt genuinely positive about Tom reaching out to his friends and starting to become more sociable again. I thought it might help to bring back the Tom I fell in love with.

However, this too came with its challenges. Tom became more focused on going out all the time; it didn't matter whether I needed him, whether we had other plans or even if we didn't have the money.

At the time, I thought it was maybe him trying to impress people and prove to his friends that he was better.

Looking back, I think it was probably in part an attempt to distract himself from how he really felt, but I also think it was a symptom in itself of how poorly he still was. I really felt invisible at this time - he was completely pushing me away but any time I tried to tell him that, an argument would ensue. Even on his birthday, when I'd made plans to treat him after work - I was totally ignored. It was my job to cook dinner and then leave him alone whilst he spent the evening playing computer games. I barely even got a grunt out of him all night.

I started to feel like I wasn't loved and truly thought he was planning to leave me. In addition to this, over the years I grew used to receiving abusive messages over Facebook from some of his friends. I generally didn't tell Tom about them because I didn't want to put him in the position of having to choose between me and his friends. However, when Tom started to receive awful messages himself, I couldn't bite my tongue any longer. Although I could understand that some of Tom's actions made others angry, it frustrated me that people felt they had the right to get involved.

Tom did things during this time which hugely impacted our relationship and took a lot of hard work for us both to accept and work through. Tom's friends knew what had happened and bombarded us with their opinions which only served to deepen the hurt I was already feeling. I had no idea what to do at this point. Tom gradually lost most of his friends, I couldn't bear

Thomas & Amber Dunning

to be near him because of the things he'd done, but yet I knew he needed me. I felt trapped and resentful. Not only that but when Tom finally decided to cut off the last few toxic friends who were making our life so difficult; they retaliated with fake Facebook profiles telling me and everyone else the gory details of what happened on the last night out they had. The only way I can describe this is like one of those awful moments where your heart sinks and you can feel yourself growing hotter, everything goes fuzzy and you don't feel like you're fully there.

I felt sick to my stomach, betrayed and terrified. I had built my entire life around living with Tom, and here it was, completely in jeopardy because of a stupid drunken decision he had made. As if that wasn't difficult enough to deal with; this all led to Tom making yet another suicide attempt.

Normally I would have done anything I could to help Tom when he was unwell. This time; however, I struggled to see past my anger. To me, at the time, Tom's tears and threats felt like a pathetic attempt to avoid the consequences of his actions. I was tired of going through the same routine with him, so I ignored much of what he said and told him that he needed to sort himself out.

That night I watched on, completely devoid of emotion as he punched holes in doors and smashed ornaments and photo frames. I felt broken and frankly didn't care what he did anymore because in my mind, things couldn't get any worse. It wasn't until he grabbed a knife and threatened to stab himself that I realised he really did need help.

114

So, not for the first time, I found myself having to swallow my pride-and my anger-and put Tom's needs first.

I wrestled the knife out of his hand and held him to stop him from grabbing it again.

Something that may have become apparent about me by now is that I was pretty risk ignorant. I would never recommend putting yourself in some of the dangerous situations that I did at times, but at that moment, I felt pretty sure that Tom would never physically harm me, and I was prepared to do whatever was necessary to keep him safe.

That said, I wouldn't do it now. Mental illness can be unpredictable and not everything you know about a person when they're well can be relied upon when they're unwell. Luckily, like the majority of people who suffer from mental illness, Tom is not violent towards others, even when he is unwell.

In fact, he is much more likely to hurt himself, which became glaringly apparent when I dared to move away from him that evening and he swiftly grabbed a screwdriver that had been knocked onto the floor and pressed it against his head. Clearly, this wasn't a situation I could manage alone.

To top off how awful that night was, amongst everything happening, my phone had died and so had Tom's. The landline had long before been smashed to pieces, and so, in a leap of faith, I ran out of the house leaving Tom alone with the screwdriver held to his temple.

Luckily my neighbours who must have been sick of the shouting by then, lent me their phone so that I could call an ambulance. I was almost too afraid to go back into the house in case he'd followed through on his threats whilst I was gone, but I knew I had to.

I sat with Tom until the triage car, made up of a paramedic and someone from the mental health team, arrived. At this point, Tom had devolved into a heap on the floor, crying, his hands covered in blood, snot literally everywhere. The triage team were truly brilliant, talked to him like he was a human and calmed him down so well; however, once again, he was left at home with me.

Looking back on this, it seems so obvious that Tom's chaotic and disinhibited behaviour was another part of his mental illness; however, we were new to this and had only really experienced the rages and outbursts; so other symptoms were easily overlooked and put down to him just making awful decisions. Not only that but we'd had such a long period of him seeming stable and had become complacent thinking that the awful part of our lives which was marked by these more explosive episodes was over.

After this latest incident, we spent weeks in shock; trying our best to recover not only the progress Tom had made with his illness but also our relationship. It meant that for the first time in a long time if we were to survive this, we would have to be honest with each other. We started to communicate, not perfectly, but better than we had before. It was tough and there were plenty of times where my resentment for what Tom had done would surface and I'd throw it in his face, but slowly we started to get back to some level of normality. Things felt settled again, but it might not be surprising to hear at this point, stability never lasted long for us.

Chapter 15 - Friends Not Friends (T)

I carried on by telling them why I had all the scars on my hands and the truth behind them. In the weeks that followed, things carried on as normal with my friends; but this was about to take a sickening turn.

I don't usually drink after my various diagnoses, but at a birthday party of one of my best friends at the time, I drank more than I usually would.

Amber and I argued about how I had ignored her all night and how my attentions were focused elsewhere. In hindsight, I did and they were, I couldn't tell at the time. I inadvertently put Amber to one side as if she didn't mean anything to me. It wasn't on purpose, I was just enveloped in my friends, not giving her a second thought, which given everything she had done for me already, she didn't deserve and is quite frankly shameful.

To make it worse, she had her reasons to not want to be left alone. Some of these so-called friends were not too keen on her, and some, I knew she felt extremely uncomfortable around, but I was blinded to this.

Not that it is true, but it seemed like I didn't care about Amber at all, as long as I was happy.

Looking back on this, to this day I hate myself for it. Amber had seen everything that went on behind the scenes; I put her through hell and yet she still wanted to stay with me and support me. The memory is easily a stain on the underpants of my life.

A full-blown argument broke out between us, I was fully in the wrong which I can now see that it was my fault in its entirety. The argument developed into something bigger because of my own stupidity and arrogance. This led me to have a psychotic episode at the party. I took off out of the house in fits of rage and sprinting down the road; I was gone.

This monstrous being was now in full control and I don't remember what happened from this point up to being back in bed with Amber cuddling me.

This would be the first time my "friends" would see me at my worst, it was one thing talking to them about it, but having them see it first-hand was something else.

The days following, Amber and I went on holiday to my mum's house as she's retired abroad and so it's just what we needed to leave life behind. It was exactly what we needed, especially at this time; but back home something was brewing which I didn't expect in the slightest.

When we came home something wasn't right. These people who I, at the time thought were my friends, were now starting to alienate me. One by one, they would not want to spend time with me – even turning down my invites to go into town for some lunch, only for me to find out that they had gone out themselves, pushing me away as if I was trash.

This progressed after a few weeks getting worse and worse; until one day their plan would come into fruition; a tirade of hatred was flowing my way, months before when I was going out all the time, a twisted and callous event occurred, something which I had kept from Amber.

I was still struggling with psychosis at that point and this "Thing" was still taking over any control

I had.

Okay, so it wasn't as frequent as it was before but still horrifying none the less. The night in question is still blank and quite frankly I wish never even happened; all I know was myself and amber had a huge fight that evening and to escape, I cowardly ran away and went into town with those "friends."

At the end of the night, I had cheated on Amber.

I took Amber's trust for granted and threw it all away. The fault was my own and no one else's, but the mental illness didn't help. That is not an excuse and please don't think I am using it as a "Get out of jail free card" – it is something which I have to own and still do.

I disgraced myself and it is still something that still makes me crumble to this day.

It wasn't long after that I saw the culmination of my friends' alienation, and without any warning, I was alerted to a fake Facebook profile made in my name from one of the very few people I still trusted. I was receiving messages from people I didn't even know saying I had been and saying certain, disgusting and revolting things.

I tried to reason with them, but I couldn't. My head was starting to spin - now Amber had to try and get these people to stop what they were doing and also tend to me. Thankfully, an old friend I had met at college, Dave, was now intervening and trying to take some of the load off of Amber understanding how twisted this was for Amber, both my actions and theirs.

In a means to end my life and the hatred which was being sent to me from those who had a huge place in my heart; I tried anything I could, I grabbed tablets which amber wrestled out of my hands; I tried to throw myself down the stairs which Amber held me back from; and finally, I grabbed a knife which my heroic better half talked me into dropping the blade on the floor, it landed millimetres away from my feet.

I didn't see anything that went on after this. It all eventually stopped, but for me, the assault continued. I couldn't get it out of my head what they had done; I couldn't figure out what to do next. I had absolutely no idea who I could trust. My hero, Amber, would never leave my side. Although she was hurting, she always ensured I was okay.

She hated me, and for good reason too. I was just as despicable as those punishing me.

Chapter 16 – Hanging on by a Thread (T)

I was hanging on for my own survival by its fingertips, I was ready to let go and fall into the darkness and delete my existence off this planet, but I was holding on for the only thing which was good in my life; Amber.

This led onto something which would stamp on my fingers and send me hurtling into what felt like oblivion.

During the lead up to the previous predicament, I was posting all my adventures online to show people I was okay (when I wasn't). You see, I don't like people worrying, even my family; so I put a lot of bravado online to demonstrate although I couldn't work, I am working on myself to get back to the usual routine of shift work – Only it wasn't seen that way. It must have been no longer than three or four days since the tidal wave of cyberbullying my once friends gave me, where I started to receive text messages – One of which still sticks on my mind and tends to repeat every so often like a terrible advertising jingle

"Don't come back, we know you're faking it."

My psyche was now in free fall into this pit of despair. I was in a nose-dive and there was no way of pulling up or grabbing onto a life-line. They were all dead to me; why couldn't people just see that I wanted to show the world I was okay? Again, going back to my old mate hindsight, being on their side of the looking glass as it were, I can see their perspective. If I could see theirs though, why couldn't they see mine?

My mind was spiralling out of control, I couldn't take it anymore. I couldn't see how Amber could help me now. Not only did I give up on any form of recovery, but I had also given up on myself.

I convinced myself of one thing: Game Over.

We were watching TV, I looked over to Amber and told her "*I love you.*"

I stood up calmly.

Grabbed the garage key and took a slow walk out.

No thoughts were in my mind.

Feeling Numb.

I opened the door and made my way to the garage. In the corner was an old goal net which had not been used since those "Friends" in a previous chapter bailed on me playing football.

I tied a knot in the ceiling joist of the garage and put a solid toolbox below me. One long step is all it took to see my next destination; Still no guardian angel giving me an alternative route or helping me to see sense last minute like it had previously…

The ligature went around my neck and tightened.

Still numb and devoid of any emotion.

Without any thoughts going through my mind and one big swing of my leg; I kicked the toolbox from out under me and gave the ligature an active test.

As it took my weight and the knot tightened, I remember the pain of it tightening and pinching my neck; only made worse while I was kicking out and putting more tension on the makeshift noose.

My vision was now in relation to my heartbeat; with every pulse, my vision came back as it was starting to progressively fade to black.

Throughout all of this, leaving the comfort of my sofa; I was not in this lucid, monstrous state where I had no control. I was still firmly at the reins of my own movements.

I was certain I did not want to be here anymore.

I was beyond desperate.

What I haven't mentioned yet, is that while I was off work, one of my coping mechanisms was to comfort eat. My weight had rocketed to twenty-three and a half stone. It would be today that obesity would save a life.

In some sick twist of fate; the ceiling joist broke. Dropping my almost lifeless body to the floor where I would remain. Gasping for breath, breaking into tears and screaming why I couldn't do it. It was set in stone for me; I had no reason for staying. I couldn't even get this right!

I couldn't put anything else on Amber, what kind of life was that? I was in complete despair and believed in all honesty, the world was better off without me.

I remember seeing a huge light shining at me as my vision was very blurry with an excess of tears and almost passing out where a shadowy figure approached me. It grabbed me and wrapped me in their embrace.

It was Amber, who simply wanted to see where I had got to. From what I remember, she expertly remained calm and held me tight to give me the ounce of comfort which I needed.

She checked me over for any injury and

immediately called for an ambulance. The usual then followed, go to the hospital, chat to the crisis team and then get sent home.

I was still in a significant level of stress and not really feeling right. I couldn't put a finger on what was wrong, but I didn't really feel anything. No love, no hatred, no shame; just neither here nor there. A bitter-sweet numbness.

This time the Crisis Team had given me some medication (Diazepam) to see me over the weekend when I could get in as an emergency appointment with the psychiatrist.

It was at this point where I should have been sectioned under the mental health act. I was a risk to my own life, but alas it never happened. Armed with a medication I'd never had before, we were ushered out to get in a taxi and return back home.

Because of this numbness, it couldn't have been more than ten minutes after we both got home, I took an overdose and walked out of the house. Amber, being the usual hero that she is, followed me, following me while I was hurtling abuse at her while I was popping this sheet of tablets like they were *tic-tacs*.

I still wasn't right. I could see and comprehend everything going on, but I wasn't in control. Everything I said to her was not meant and it was horrific some of the expletives which were being thrown her way, but she never left my side.

I was manically laughing. It was like one of these voices took over and wanted to make its presence known.

I remember I eventually turned around, walked past her and then back home. I screamed that I had taken an overdose, and again, as cool as she was after my first failed suicide attempt, called an ambulance. It was in the ambulance where I regained some form of control.

It hit me as if someone had thrown a brick of reality at my forehead, everything from senses and emotions came back at once.

My neck felt like it was burning from the rope burn I had gotten beforehand, I realised everything I said to Amber. I turned to face her and I truly saw her; exhausted, make-up running down her face, red-eyed. This made compounded the feeling of guilt already surrounding me.

I could see how much I'd hurt her now. I couldn't live with myself.

I just wanted to die.

I walked into A&E, where I took my seat; with Amber by my side. Holding me tight; as if she was never going to let go. I knew there and then; she was going to be with me no matter what; I don't think I would have been able to stay around if I was in her position – it was a miracle she was still here at all!

I was called into the Triage office to see the same nurse I'd seen after attempting to hang myself. I could see from the desperation in her eyes that she wanted to help but was powerless. I think even she knew I was living on borrowed time. I had to have blood tests to ensure that the overdose hadn't caused any permanent damage.

While I was waiting, I begged Amber to not let them put in in a hospital unit. I needed Amber even if it meant I was confined to the bedroom or the house in general. The crisis team walked through and took me into the office. I understood their frustrations, but even then, they seemed lost on what to do.

The person who had seen me twice in one night

callously said: "*I guess you've gobbled up all those tablets then!*"

It was said in such a seemingly wicked way that I thought the crisis team had it all planned; like it was a paranoid scheme that even the crisis team wanted me done with. My deluded thoughts directed me to think that those people I once cared about had told the crisis team to end my life.

They asked if I would voluntarily go into the care of the hospital or the crisis house, but I flat out refused. "*No.*" I refused bluntly. They turned to Amber.

"*I think he's better with me. I'm safe don't worry*" Amber said to the support worker. The choice ultimately wasn't mine, it was simply asked to give the illusion and comfort that I had some say in the matter. This time we were given no medications and sent home. The next few days saw me stay at home and isolate myself away.

Every time someone came to the door, or someone saw me; I was convinced they knew exactly what was going on and how I was a disgrace, a waste on critical emergency services, and worse making it up to get attention.

Going into A&E because of mental distress was enough to solidify the thought of '*I have let everyone and myself down*' but going twice in one night because I had tried to take my life, made me feel like I had hit the bottom of the metaphorical barrel. It felt like I was beyond help.

This was my life now and it was a matter of time until my luck ran out and either Amber left me or I would finally succeed in taking my life.

Whenever I did venture out of the house and attempt to go into town to pick up a book or even just some groceries, I would spy around every corner to make sure my ex so-called friends were nowhere to be seen.

Every time I entered a shop my heartbeat increased rapidly and I would often just burst into tears; what if I see them? Would I be controllable, or would I enter the same fit of rage like back in school where I would take out all my emotions on them and get in a huge fight?

I would be lying if I said I didn't want to hurt them – I wanted revenge so badly but there was no limit to the level of hurt I would put on them for what they had put me through, and there was no way I could let Amber suffer the fallout of these actions.

Chapter 17- In the dark (A)

One evening, Tom and I were cuddled up on the sofa watching a film when he got up, said he needed to get something out of the garage, kissed me and told me he loved me. I'm going to assume that you've already read Tom's side of this and so know what happens next and with that in mind, it would be easy to wonder - how did I not notice something was wrong? Doesn't it look like he's saying goodbye? Well, no; it didn't. Tom and I trade "*I love yous*" like they're oxygen. We always have. And Tom had always been the sort to remember last minute that he needed to do something, so this scenario for us was something that happened often.

Ten minutes passed and as the film ended, I realised that Tom hadn't returned. Normally this wouldn't have bothered me but something didn't feel right. I can only describe it as a general feeling of unease, but nothing urgent.

Feeling somewhat inconvenienced actually, I went out to the garage. I fully expected to see him tinkering with something as he often did, and figured I'd just check how long he'd be and go back inside. The scene I was met with when I got to the door was completely different.

A sight that I wasn't prepared for. Tom was on the floor with something - I genuinely don't remember what -around his neck. I could see he was awake and breathing but he was holding onto the ligature he'd made, keeping it tight around his throat like he was desperate to choke out every bit of oxygen he could. I ran over and grabbed his hands, trying to loosen the ligature.

Tom has always been significantly stronger than me; so prying his hands free was one of the most physically challenging things I've ever had to do. I actually think the only reason I managed to loosen his grip was that he was losing consciousness, so his ability to fight against me was reduced. I pulled the make-shift noose off him and held him tight.

It's hard for me to say how I felt at this point because adrenaline had kicked in and I was completely on autopilot.

You're never taught what to do if you find someone trying to ligate themselves- even on the suicide intervention course I'd been on months earlier- I knew ways to try and prevent it but not what you're meant to do if you actually see it happening. It wasn't until we arrived at A&E in the ambulance that I really allowed myself to think about what had happened.

My first memory is overwhelmingly of fear. I could have lost him that night and the thought of facing a future without Tom makes my heart hurt.

Even now, thinking about that is one of the few things through this whole awful time that makes me cry. I was scared for him - I didn't know what this would mean - would he need to stay in hospital? What would we tell his family? Would he try to do it again once we were home?

It would be understandable if I'd felt angry that he'd done this to me, but I can honestly say I never did.

I've seen too many people try to self-harm and

end their lives through my work in mental health that I understand the deep sadness and desperation someone has to feel to reach that point and looking across at Tom in the A&E waiting room, his pain was visible, and I could feel it too.

I had so many things running through my mind, but I was also relieved that even for a few moments, he was safe.

We repeated our usual process of being checked over in triage and then waiting to see the crisis team. Every other time we'd been to the hospital I had accompanied Tom in his conversations with them; however, this time, as I stood up to walk into the side room with him, a hand gently stopped me and I was told: "*we'd rather talk to him on his own so he can talk to us openly.*"

Now don't get me wrong, I understood their reasons and have seen enough relatives of patients in my own time working in the field to know that sometimes they can get in the way. I am also fully accepting of the fact that Tom didn't, doesn't and never will tell me every last thing-I wouldn't want him to. However, I also knew Tom. I knew that he was scared of hospitalisation and would lie to avoid it. This was a man who had casually kissed me moments before trying to hang himself; I knew he wouldn't think twice about pretending he was fine to get out of the hospital. Barely an hour passed and Tom was back; I was told he'd been given some medication to help him and that he was to return home tonight and that his Psychiatrist would be informed.

That was it. Tom wouldn't talk to me, and I had no idea what the medication was, how much he had, or what frame of mind he was in. Once home we went straight to bed and Tom took one of the tablets, shortly after he walked out of the bedroom. Worried, I asked where he was going. "*What's it to you*?" He snapped. He then started rambling about things that made no sense at all and when I told him he was acting strange he responded with "*fuck it, I've had enough of this*" and disappeared down the stairs and out the front door. Wearing just my pyjamas with nothing on my feet I rushed after him. When I think back to the next half an hour or so, I picture it sped up a little with the Benny Hill theme playing in the background.

I chased Tom around the local estate as he took tablet after tablet, throwing the empty packets behind him, laughing, telling me there was nothing I could do to stop him. I don't know whether it was his adrenaline or my own lack of fitness but no matter how fast I ran I could never quite catch up with his walk. I was screaming for him to stop and come home, desperately saying anything I could to calm him down. I was terrified because I had no idea what he had taken or what the effects would be on him.

Thankfully, he did eventually return home, and I called our second ambulance that night.

Back in A&E, I felt so angry about what had happened and if I'm honest, I still do. I think this could have been prevented. If I'd been allowed to stay with him the first time he saw the crisis team, I could have told them how I didn't feel he was safe to go home; how I didn't think I could cope with being his only support that night.

At the very least, I would have known what medication he had on him and could have asked questions about how to keep him safe. Instead, I had been kept in the dark and had only a man who we later learned was in psychosis to provide me with any information. This time, we both saw the crisis team together, but the interaction lasted all of five minutes. Their advice to a man who had attempted to hang and overdose himself in a matter of hours was to go home and sleep off the tablets he'd "gobbled up". Understandably, this served to make me feel even angrier and above all, let down.

I realised at this point that I had a bigger battle on our hands than the one to keep Tom alive.

I was also fighting to be involved in his care as his carer. Quite rightly, mental health care is focussed on trying to help patients to get better in the community, avoiding hospitalisation wherever possible. This, however, combined with a lack of funding for vital community resources, means that we carers can often find ourselves delivering the bulk of our loved ones support alone.

We're the ones who find ourselves having to put in place safety measures, recognise the signs of relapse and calling for emergency help when our loved ones are too unwell to do this themselves.

It makes perfect sense, therefore, that we should also be included in the important care decisions that are made.

I understand that every patient has the right to confidentiality, and Tom was at the time deemed to have the capacity to make his own decisions too.

I feel strongly that professionals, even if they can't disclose information, should ask present family and friends what their experience of their loved one's mental health is as this can provide valuable insight into what life for the patient is like outside of the small glimpse into their world that a professional can get from a patient during their consultation.

Had I been asked about my experience with Tom's mental health by any health care professional we met along the way; I could have told them about all the times I wrestled scissors or knives out of his hands, the times I blocked his punches from hitting a door or his head from hitting a wall. I could have told them about the hours spent wondering where he was when he would disappear threatening to end his life. I could have told them about the panic attacks I had suffered as a result of the helplessness and fear I had fought back for months.

Tom couldn't tell them those things because he didn't remember most of them, and I was careful not to tell him too much in an effort to lessen the guilt I knew he already felt.

Perhaps I could have made a difference in the support we received had I challenged the mental health teams, but I worked alongside many of them in the jobs that I did, and was worried that if I challenged anything, it would impact on my work.

The only time I ever did stand up and fight our corner was after Tom had started hallucinating that there was blood on his hands on the way back from the cinema.

I had called 111 that night in the hope that they could send the crisis team; however, they couldn't and insisted that they would send an ambulance to take us to A&E to see them instead. With very few other options as we were stranded in a layby in the middle of nowhere, I sat with Tom and waited. I am not a confrontational person, and I would never dream of arguing with any professional within our emergency services; however, I stand by my actions in the minutes that followed the arrival of our ambulance.

I felt relieved when the paramedic arrived, but this quickly turned to confusion as he sat in his car for a further 5 minutes. I got out of our car and walked over to him, at which point he started to ask me what had happened.

I explained about Tom's hallucinations and that we needed help to get to A&E.

"He's in the car, couldn't he drive himself?" The paramedic scoffed.

I was gobsmacked. *"Do you really think it would be safe for a man who is hallucinating to drive?"* I asked. *"What if he caused an accident?"* Clearly still not understanding the severity of the situation, the paramedic then asked,

"Well, why couldn't you have called a taxi?"

At this point Tom was crying uncontrollably, convinced he was covered in blood, he was staring at his hands and when you tried to talk to him, he didn't even seem to hear you. I wasn't sure I could have even got him out the car, never mind convinced any taxi driver to pick up a man in that state.

I explained this as calmly as I could, and so the paramedic approached the car, got in the passenger side and started to talk to Tom, and then, when Tom didn't respond, he started to become irritated, scolding him with,

"I can't help you if you aren't even going to talk to me."

At this point, I saw red and demanded that he got out of the car. I raised my voice and said, *"Look, I know you see some awful things, and you clearly don't want to help him, so before you make him worse, I want you to leave. I'd rather call his dad and wait the hour for him to get here than take up any more of your time. I'll just have to find a way to keep him safe."*

For what felt like forever, there was nothing but silence, until the paramedic looked up and apologised. He explained that he'd driven all the way from Boston and was tired and that if we would like, he would take us to A&E. Poor excuse, I thought, but I desperately wanted Tom to get the help he needed.

The paramedic apologised further in the ambulance after I'd explained some of the things that had happened over the years, and from that point, treated us respectfully. I didn't take it further because I genuinely believe that health care professionals have enough to deal with without having to defend complaints. I hope that our interaction was enough to make him at least fake more compassion with the next mental health patient he attends.

I think a lot more can be done to not only increase a professional's understanding of mental health problems; and also, to educate people on the impact of mental illness on carers. There were times whereby not giving me important information about Tom's care, they put me under more pressure and him at more risk. After all, how was I ever meant to keep him safe if I wasn't given any of the information? To that end, I also wholeheartedly encourage those with mental illness to have a discussion with anyone in their support network around what each of their needs and wishes are.

Open communication between patients, professionals and carers can be the difference between life and death and can also mean that should a patient lack the capacity to make decisions about their own care, those who support them can communicate their wishes to professionals on their behalf.

Even something as simple as giving the services you're involved with permission to speak to your carer can mean that both parties can share enough information to keep you and your carer safe and supported.

The result of this can only be that everyone feels more supported and more capable of managing mental illness in the community which in turn can only mean better outcomes for patients.

Chapter 18 – A new road opens. (T)

During the time where I had started to isolate myself, Amber would attend a support group for carers run by the charity "Rethink." This was every two weeks and she could meet people who are in the same boat as her, i.e. caring for a partner with mental health issues.

She would learn all about various mental health issues and relative disorders to help in the care of those afflicted; it was also a good respite for her too, where she could socialise and essentially have a night off from what I kept throwing her way.

After I received my various diagnosis', Amber told me about an evening where a mental health professional would be talking to the carers group, and how it may be of interest.

Now at first, I really didn't want to go; She went on to say that other people would be there with the same diagnosis which just fortified my position that I didn't want to be subjected to this.

"*No*." I fired at Amber.

I couldn't get off the thought that this would affirm to me that I was beyond help. Seeing other people with the same symptoms still struggling would be so degrading for me and I knew it would set me back to the very beginning.

I had a long think.

The anxiety in me was going into overdrive, I could feel a full-on panic attack brewing like a storm in the distance and I'm floundering around in the grand expanse of the ocean.

I took my medication of Propranolol and thought about it some more. It took some convincing on my own part, but I eventually settled for a decision.

A few hours later; *"Okay, I'll do it."* I replied to Amber.

I'm going to go; not for me but for Amber and our relationship. If, and it's a big if, this could stop the love of my life being subjected to the horrific emotional torment I was inadvertently throwing her way – she would be happy again.

On the way to the evening's event, I firmly believed that all this session would do would be to reaffirm that I was beyond help. Solidifying the thoughts that I was not normal and that this illness was going to take over my life to the extent of having no future, and no further career progression.

It's amazing where there are little moments where your whole life just seems to make a complete U-turn and change direction.

I left the session feeling hugely empowered.
I met people who had the exact same diagnosis I had and yet were CEO's of their own companies; they owned their own businesses or were moving up the management ladder and for once, in this long old run to recovery there it was. Hope!

I had a smile.

"I'm not beyond help."

I found that I could finally look forward to my life with some kind of positivity.

A new fire was burning deep within; I was starting to feel passionate about progressing myself not only at work but how I could feel proud about seeking help.

The realisation that mental illness was actually a normal, natural and common thing was sobering and injected a good dose of normality into my conscious. I finally felt like I was not the only one who was suffering, waiting for life to just take me.

I look back and I feel so pathetic because of my denial of anything being wrong, pushing every emotion to one side and in turn cause so much distress to my family and friends because of what I was going through.

My love for life was now starting to gather momentum after being on hold and stagnant for what felt like an eternity.

I could feel something rising within me like a phoenix rising from its ashes, spreading its wings to take flight in the next stage of its life.

I was getting stronger and more resilient in myself. My issues were still there but rather than being prominent, they were now just an underlay of what my new flooring has been built upon.

It was time to rebuild my life.

First things first; Return to work.

That first day, I felt like some sordid secret and the dirt on the bottom of a shoe as I walked in.

I took a deep breath and walked into the factory. I got changed and then took a seat in the office waiting for the team to assemble for the morning meeting.

One by one people filtered into the room, took one look at me said "hi" and then took their own place.

Not a word was said, I could tell everyone was looking at each other not knowing what to say in case I took anything the wrong way.

You could cut the tension with a knife.

The door swung open and one of the more outspoken, funny employees walked through the door.

He took one look at me.

"*NOW THEN POLAR BEAR!*" – he expressed.

Everyone laughed. Not like the usual comical laugh but the laugh of shock, like when you say to someone "*You can't say that!*"

"*Hi mate. Uhhh, why polar bear?*" – I quizzed him

"*Well, your bipolar; part man – part bear. Polar Bear!*" – he explained.

Well, I couldn't fault his logic I suppose, except I wasn't suffering from bipolar disorder, it kind of proved to me that there were all sorts of rumours flying around about me. This would be my first test. I was surrounded by people who had sent me those hateful messages all that time ago, and I was now being faced with Chinese whispers ricocheting around the workplace. This would be a huge steppingstone. However, I didn't feel insulted or targeted.

I found myself in hysterics and so happy that someone at least is confident to mock me in such a jovial and friendly manner. It made me feel part of the team again, and finally in a place where I could fit back in. I knew it would take time before I would be back in everyone's good books, but this fire that had been ignited just a few weeks ago made me want to progress. I was still receiving therapy through CBT and I attended these sessions religiously. This kept adding fuel to help strengthen the flame of passion and positive outlook I now had in my life and I could now apply the techniques I had learnt in these sessions to my life.

Chapter 19- Getting better (A)

Whilst I'd been helping Tom to battle his own mental health problems, I'd started to develop issues of my own. I became anxious and depressed. Some of my behaviours became obsessive, for example, it would take me a good five minutes to wash one fork because I had to wash, then visually check, then wash, then check with my hands for debris and then wash again because I'd touched it. Soon, it became easier to use disposable plates and cutlery. I think for me, so much was out of my control in my life, that I needed to find ways of controlling other areas of my life. I think there was also an element of having fallen so far behind with housework due to everything that was going on, that I over-compensated with the things I used daily like cutlery and the shower. I also became extremely self-conscious, started cancelling plans and spent much of my time either at work or in bed. Some days, I'd feel too anxious to even go into our kitchen because it was directly opposite that of our neighbour and I was scared that if anyone saw me, they would try to speak to me.

I saw my GP, started on anti-depressants and was referred to our local talking-therapies service. I was sceptical at first about how these would help and was apprehensive about revealing everything that had happened. Things I'd kept secret for so long. However, as soon as I was greeted by my lovely therapist, I felt at ease.

At first, we worked more generally on my anxiety and over time, I trusted her enough to tell her about what had been happening at home.

My therapist asked if I would mind her putting me in touch with Rethink who could support me in my caring role. I agreed and shortly after I received a call from an amazing woman called Trish who talked me through the support on offer and invited me to an appointment.

I fought every urge to cancel that appointment and went, and I am so glad I did! Trish did a carers assessment with me and gave me some general tips on how to support Tom but with boundaries that protected my own wellbeing. She also invited me to a support group. The group was carers only and was made up of the most welcoming, brave and supportive people I have ever met. Every two weeks we would meet and cover different subjects from medication and break-away techniques to how to be more involved in our loved one's care, all over a hot chocolate and some cake. It was the space and understanding I had needed for so long!

I continued my therapy, and after a while was stepped up for further CBT which consisted mostly of graded exposure. I gradually learned to manage and control my symptoms and over time expose myself to my triggers whilst reducing my less helpful behaviours, eventually, bringing things under control. While I notice that some of the tendencies I have seem to creep back when I'm stressed or anxious, I know now how to stop it from spiralling; and I also now have more helpful ways to manage my anxiety whenever it pops up.

Although I'd gained some control over my own issues, home life continued to be strained.

Tom was still to some degree avoiding addressing his underlying mental health problem. His suicide attempt had only compounded the shame he felt and it was like he was going through the motions from one appointment to the next, never really identifying as someone with a mental illness. The group I was attending invited us both to a presentation by a lead Pharmacist in mental health. I had made friends with one of the women at the group whose husband had a very similar story to Tom and I knew he would be going, so over the next two weeks, I pestered and pestered Tom until he reluctantly agreed to come.

That night changed everything. Tom met people who were business owners; others who had survived suicide and their loved ones who had stood by them throughout. He saw that there were others just like him, that there was a light at the end of the tunnel and that mental illness didn't make him any less capable or any less lovable. I will be forever thankful to the therapist who put me in touch with that group. I'm lucky enough to have been able to thank her since. It was this night where our lives really started to change for the better. Tom became more actively involved in trying to get better. He started to take care of himself again, started to talk more, and gradually with the help of medication and therapy, I could see him returning to the man I'd fallen in love with. We still had a long way to go; Tom's experiences with his former friends had made him anxious to put himself out into the world again but at least in our small bubble, things were improving.

The next couple of years were a blur of psychiatrist appointments, waiting lists and medication changes.

Eventually, Tom got to see the Early Interventions in Psychosis team who started to shed some light on why Tom was having the experiences he'd suffered over the last few years.

Gaining the insight that his current mental illness was likely due to not having dealt with the death of his brother at least gave Tom a starting point. It gave him something to focus on and begin to work through; and it gave me the hope that perhaps by addressing his unresolved grief and dealing with traumatic events; there could be a future where Tom wouldn't have to suffer in this way.

Slowly we started to manage the various parts of his illness. Together we created him a flow chart of "*what to do when I feel like this*". This was broken down into his mild, moderate and more urgent symptoms. We never really used the chart itself but having the conversation about what to do at certain times really helped to feel in control and like we were prepared. I installed various apps onto Tom's phone which had a number of self-help tools that he could use.

We communicated more, argued less and tried to enjoy life as much as we could whilst being careful not to miss any signs of a relapse. Tom stabilised on his medication and for the first time in a long time, I felt like I could finally relax and be a partner, not a carer.

Although this was a good thing, this was such a weird feeling. I was so used to having to be hypervigilant, alert to any signs of change, that I found it difficult to switch off that carer side of me. To be honest, I always will. When the person you care for gets better, you don't stop being a carer. There's always a part of you that is acutely aware that things could change in an instant; but over time, I have learnt to make the most of the freedom we have from this awful illness. We started to explore our interests and passions, to see more of the world, trying new things...it was like we were a brand-new couple, treading this path for the first time. It felt like the fresh start we both needed.

Chapter 20 – Bouncing back. (T)

The subsequent two years from the previous chapter had flown by. I was still getting the odd hiccup regarding my mental health, but these were coming few and far between.

The voices were still intrusive, but the medications kept them at bay and helped to maintain such sound cognitive stability that I could see what was real and what was just a figment of my imagination. I was armed and ready to protect myself and my own honour was now fully restored, although still supported with the odd bit of scaffolding here and there.

I was still struggling to get out to the world and I was fairly lonely but because that's how I wanted it to be, I still wanted to limit the external variables which could cause me any issues in my own mind. This is when Amber came up with an idea.

She enlisted the help of Billy, the very same billy from at a decade previous who was the extra piece in our "Airband" and suggested why don't we start making media together like we used to back in school. Amber knew of our podcasting days because although it was something myself and Billy enjoyed, it was something I was so proud of, I think it was the first thing amber knew about me!

I got back in touch with him as Amber suggested, and there it was; like "Queen" forming after the band "Smile" – we founded the "Win of the week." Podcast, little did we know that this would be the start of something big!

"*Watch out world, we are coming for you*!" – I thought to myself.

When we had lived together before my mental health became an issue, we were toying with this idea of making a YouTube series, but it never really gained momentum.

One-night Billy asked me if I minded if his cousin were to join us one evening – I would soon come to realise that this would lead on to something great. Triple Mega Super Threat.

The win of the week podcast was limited to just Billy and me, getting a bottle of alcohol and slowly getting progressively drunk while trying to make sense of the week's politics, media and everything in between; but it was evolving.

The three of us; Billy, his cousin Alan and me (All of us from Cornwall originally – bonus points!) came together and decided that if we were serious about doing this, we needed a re-vamp. We need a re-birth.

Looking around the room we were all flummoxed on what name to pick, let's just say creativity wasn't our strong point.

"*Billy, I want us to have a name like an over the top game show…*" I suggested, essentially begging to get us off the starting blocks.

"…*How about this*?" Billy responded.

He held up a piece of paper.

We all looked at each other and in unison said "*YES!*"

TRIPLE MEGA SUPER THREAT!!!!

Written in capitals, bold and more than its fair share of exclamation points. This would be something great, well maybe not so great in the grand scheme of things, but for my own development great!

The podcast was just an evolution of "The win of the week" but it was now three guys, talking everything from movies, TV, video games and beyond.

It took weeks to get the foundations set, we invested in new equipment – mixers, microphones and even a new laptop for recording onto.

A few episodes in and we gelled, we connected like the last three pieces of a jigsaw puzzle. Within the first three episodes, we were a force to be reckoned with.

We were even starting to get some recognition in the form of fan mail. People loved us and what we were doing! More importantly, I was pouring out my soul online and being my open self in front of two friends and to the world and people wanted more!

I finally felt acceptance.

Acceptance! Something I thought long gone after the battery of abuse and bullying I had faced... We even reached the iTunes top 100 podcasts! All for about 10 minutes but that wasn't the point. People loved us, and people I have never met loved me, for me.

Unfortunately, Billy (being in the armed forces) got posted and that left me and Alan to continue the show. We just couldn't balance our schedules to give the show the required focus it deserved and so, the project came to its natural conclusion.

This new abundance of time I now had, was to play havoc with my mind.

I was starting to get a bit flippant at home, not in the extreme as it used to be with smashing the house up but Amber and I would progressively enter more and more arguments.

We agreed I needed a new project, something new to

focus on and allow me to really challenge myself.

Within months, Amber and I went full wedding planning mode!

The time was creeping up quicker than we could ever imagine and we had so much to do. It's amazing; as soon as you mention the word wedding to any supplier or venue the price shoots right up!! These months, as I said flew past and finally came our wedding day.

Amber was busy getting ready while Mum and I went to set up the venue.

My best man was none other than Billy, back on leave and the excitement was starting to kick in. Family and friends from all over the UK had come to witness our marriage and for once I had the concrete proof of the love and support, not only of my lover but my best friend in my life.

I was stood at the front awaiting my bride to walk down the aisle and then the music played.

Anxiety like I have never felt before in my life.

My heart felt like it had stopped but immediately shot back into action; trying to keep up with what it had missed.

The music being provided by a barbershop-quartet singing the smooth melody of "God only knows" by the beach boys.

Out walked Amber looking absolutely incredible, I couldn't believe I was going to spend the rest of my life with this amazing woman, the absolute love of my life.

The day went off without a hitch; surrounded in love, happiness, family and friendship. It was perfect, even if Amber tried to give me a heart attack by saying my middle name when exchanging our vows instead of my first!

Amber and I were married and now I was raring for a new challenge. This is where we set upon my new project.

I was going to lose weight.

I was significantly overweight and classed as obese; I would look at myself in the mirror and although I was starting to like that I was looking after myself and my own image, my physical health wasn't exactly brilliant.

Our diet consisted of takeaway every night. Now to some; this would sound like paradise. Chinese one night, pizza the next; then a curry and then back to the ol' faithful Chinese, but trust me, you soon feel the drawbacks of this lifestyle. My weight skyrocketed. It's amazing how nutrition and diet play an active role in mental health. I felt lethargic, unable to do anything and although this fire I keep mentioning – the passion for life – was still enflamed; it was hard to actually do anything physical. I dreaded moving, getting up in the morning and I genuinely just felt fed up all the time. It wasn't that I didn't feel like I wanted to be around, I was neither happy nor sad, I just felt contempt with everything, and I found myself snapping at people and getting into more disagreements. I was holding my own body in a poor posture too and I was generally physically not in a great place.

Looking back on my teens when I played basketball, I looked thin, and well I thought I was even slightly good looking; but when I look in a mirror now, all I saw was a damaged, emotionally scarred, fat lump. That night, I invested in a cheap pair of trainers and running clothes to get me started. I signed up to a gym which was open 24 hours – this would be a significant investment given I was working a rolling pattern of nights and days, so it was always accessible. The gear eventually turned up on my front door and I couldn't wait to get out and go for a run.

Still suffering the effects of the bullying, I had serious issues leaving the house. Just the thought of walking outside was enough to make my heart jump out of my chest. I knew I had to do this; this was the time I was going to change my own life for the better – A change that I NEEDED to make.

I took one deep breath, put my headphones in, Sunglasses. The door swung open and out I leapt like a young springbok.

That first run, it truly nearly killed me – but in a good way! An activity where I could just lace up my trainers, put my headphones in and go wherever the pavement wanted to take me. This was soon to become an obsession.

I started to eat better and go running daily, trying to better my own times and improve my own health.

The weight started to drop off quite fast, but always I made sure that I was healthy in doing so. If I was going to do this, I was going to do it properly. When those trainers were on and the music was in, I felt myself disengage from the world and its troubles, I had an invisible bubble protecting me, like sonic the hedgehog with one of his powerups.

I was in my own little world and I was loving it. Even when on some days I would run past those who wronged me, bullied more and lied about me all those years ago and yes, I would feel the anger and the betrayal anew; but I was 100% in control. I would not let anger get a foothold again.

I simply ran past and carried on. I was in my happy place; a place where the external stimuli of the socially diseased and corrupt world of hatred couldn't get to me.

After every run I would, of course, be tired, but not where I would be snappy, groggy or a horror to be around – I was smiling, happy and infected with runners high!

I recorded all my runs on the fitness apps which were available at the time and ensured I could keep a track on how my fitness was progressing and gradually improving.

The words "*I feel sad*" never came out of my mouth, never mind even enter my mind and in actual fact, I was feeling the exact opposite.

I was starting to love looking in the mirror. Stone by stone, Kilogram by Kilogram the weight dropped off me – It would be this point where I would Inadvertently start **MENTAL HEALTH RUNNER**. It started as a simple Instagram account under my own name, and nothing more. I simply decided to record my progression, mainly to upload to Facebook so everyone could see what I was doing and that I was bouncing back from the void.

One by one people sent me messages saying how much of an inspiration I was to people trying to lose weight and make a positive change to their life.

I was making new friends and more and more "likes" and "Followers" started coming to my page.

Eventually, 8 months had flown by where I ran, I ate healthily and lived the life I had wanted years ago and I met my target weight of 16 stone (101.6Kg). I lost seven and a half stone (47.1 Kg) by doing nothing overly strenuous but just loving my life and loving what I was doing.

I broke into tears. I had done it. I looked at myself in the mirror and compare myself to where I had been a few months ago and how such a short amount of time in the grand scheme of things can change my life and even how much better I looked.

Not only looking healthy but I looked confident.

This fire for life was now a furnace and it was rewarding me with confidence, passion and love.
This is when it hit me, like a sucker punch across the chops – At no point in this journey had I ever felt stressed, depressed or even hatred towards myself.
I heard no voices; I saw no illusions.

I felt cured of what was previously an array of incurable mental health disorders and a by-product of the exercise was enhanced mental health.
This is when my new project was born. Much like a child out of the womb; a product of passion, love and dedication.

"Mental Health Runner" was born.

Chapter 21 – The present day (T).

Now I felt stable in my own issues and applying everything I had learnt in the sessions with the various therapists, I could look back on my life, my troubled journey through mental health and how far I'd come.

That left me with a troubling and perplexing thought though…

If I had known more about mental health and the issues sufferers face; could this have all be avoided?

I knew nothing in relation to mental health before it happened to me. The way I look back on it is that you wouldn't go on a long drive without making sure your car would make it; or, you wouldn't go for a walk in an alien country without looking at a map.

Why is mental health any different?

I wanted this to change, I needed this to change and it was for those reasons I launched myself into a project designed to bring mental health education to the public. I knew how big and important this was to me, I didn't realise how big and important it was to others.

I had thought about doing some form of mental health awareness following the success in my weight loss and how I felt running had played such a significant role in keeping my head on the straight and narrow.

Facing the facts though, I didn't really have any knowledge in how sport and mental health are intrinsically linked, but I had proven in my own progress on how it could play a vital and pivotal role. My mother was visiting from abroad and we got into a discussion on how far I'd come and the weight I'd lost. I asked her as a professional in the mental health support field, if my story was worth being shared? She said "*It's still a subject no one really likes to talk about*" something which reverberated within me and struck a sharp chord - She was right!

With Mum's background within the mental health sector, you would have thought she would be the first person I would have gone to for help. In simple terms, I couldn't. I didn't want her to feel like she had to leave work or feel like she had to worry. I didn't tell her a thing about what I was going through and it wouldn't be until I was in a half-decent state of recovery. I still felt like I needed to protect her from the harsh reality I was facing – she knew nothing about it.

She was absolutely correct.

I had no reply to her statement but the question that never left my mind was – "*Why?*"
See if you had an injury, it could be a black eye or having a cast on a broken limb, you will always be asked "*What happened?*" or "*Can I sign your cast?*" why shouldn't it be the same for mental health? And the root cause is blatantly obvious.

No one knows enough about mental health and many rely on media stereotypes branding us insane or unpredictably violent. Ensuring that mental health is kept taboo and not talked about openly.

I felt a great need to change this.

The answer to the question which lingered in the back of my mind which I mentioned earlier – "*If I had known more about mental health and the issues sufferers face; could this have all been avoided?*"

The date was 1st of June 2017; I had finally started a project which would follow me to this present day:

Mental Health Runner.

Mental health runner was simply a name I had come up with; I'm hardly creative as it is and naming things is no different!

I decided to turn my Instagram name from my own to the same as my blog to give a link from the social media platform to that of the newly created website and I was away!

I thought it would be hard; bringing back all my stories, the pain, the stresses and in some respects it was.

I would be lying if I said it gets easier, for me it doesn't but the CBT has taught me not to look back in anger or look back in hatred; but to try and consider them as a building block to a recovery, where I am now and what it has made me.

Sharing my stories and life lessons on the internet, I left myself wide open to any negative comments and this initially drove my anxiety wild. I couldn't help but think that those who sent me those messages all those months ago would make their opinions heard again and kill the project before it had even begun.

Resilience would be a skill I needed if I wanted to continue. I felt like I was wading through a quagmire of hatred, unknown and sadness and, always I must keep my head above the silt ridden water if I was to get this blog going.

I had no idea at this point that my own mental health was now supported massively on my own life lessons, morals and truths which I had no choice but to go through; it only strengthened my desire to help those who need it most.

I found my Instagram followers start to explode in numbers, I got messages of thanks and how they were using my story to help not only themselves but their partners going through the same things I did. I was receiving fan mail and all I was doing was talking! My passion for exercise, mental health awareness and my own physical health saw me in a local 5-a-side team, allowing me a different outlet to just running and preventing boredom or stagnation.

I would don my favourite team (Rochdale AFC) kit and be one of those who turned up in the full strip every week, thinking he was the next Ronaldo, only to be the Emile Heskey of the football team!

I was asked one Thursday to help a team by the league organisers and so I thought I would go down and see what I could do. It never occurred to me that I would end up playing a role in saving someone's life.

It was a fairly good game of football after the first 20 minutes was up, half time was called and as a team, we regrouped to devise a plan to win the match. As we kicked off the second half, our goalkeeper Michael shouted to the opposition "*Is your mate alright?*"

It was as if this was a signal and the chap in question took this as his cue, dropped to the floor.

"*S**T!*" – Michael and I said in shock

Michael straight away went to his aid while I sprinted into the sports centre to ask for help. I was back within moments and saw my teammate performing CPR .

We learnt that his name was Lucas, a young lad who you would not expect to have any physical issues and was extremely athletic.

Michael continued CPR and I could see he was tiring. I took over the compressions ensuring our fallen colleague could get air into his system.

Time slowed, and something took over.

Rather than this pent up rage monster coming out and doing its best impression of King-Kong, this "Thing" had control and was doing good!

My CPR skill had never been tested on an actual person, only on the lifeless dummy when I was on a course at 19 years of age, and that was nine years ago!

We cycled the responsibility to ensure all our energy was put into the compressions to support his life.

We both bellowed out in unison to stop all the games and get off the pitch. The league referees all agreed and ushered all those not important to the carpark.

The sound of Lucas's breathing air in and out while we were doing compressions was haunting. I'll never forget the sound.

The ambulance service turned up and was setting up all the monitoring equipment while we carried on taking turns with CPR.

Auto-pilot took over – It wasn't causing me any distress or attacking me; just wanted to help save someone's life.

The paramedics shocked Lucas once; we carried on compressions as his heart started to come back into rhythm.

As soon as it came back, it stopped. Shocked again, then back onto the compressions and he was back – this time he was stable. The paramedics and first responders took Lucas away and as quickly as he was in the back of the ambulance, the vehicle was gone into the distance to the nearest hospital leaving its trail blazed with blue light.

I turned to Lucas's teammates.

All understandably wanted to go to the hospital to wait for him and I was not going to get in their way.

I gave my mobile number to one of the players so he could give me a call or a text to update me on Lucas' condition, and off they went.

Michael was in the sports centre, I walked into the carpark to be greeted with people shaking my hand while a chorus of clapping encircled us.

I could do nothing but say thanks, get in the car and go home; I was tired from football, never mind the compressions we had to do-it's surprising how tiring it is in real life.

About halfway home the reality of what has just happened hit me.

I may have saved someone's life, me, who by rights should not have even been alive at this point! I pulled over - projectile vomited into the River Witham.

I got home, told Amber everything that happened and just burst into tears. It would be days until I felt normal in my own skin.

It felt like I had just had a psychotic episode and that I was being looked at and judged by everyone around me. I had done good, except feeling the polar opposite. This was a foreign emotion; I had no idea how or what to feel.

That night I received a text saying that Lucas was awake, his short-term memory was shot, for the time being, he could remember people faces and those who were important in his life.

Now you may be thinking after reading this that I have gone on a two-page tangent which this doesn't really apply to anything – but on the contrary!

This helping save someone's life. It wasn't easy, much like in the respect of saving my own but in a different capacity. I had so many similar connotations, that it opened new thought patterns for me.

So back to the question I asked myself previously once I set up my blog:

"If I had known more about mental health and the issues suffers face; could this have all be avoided?"

This question doesn't just apply to mental health. If I had no skills in CPR or basic first aid, would this have had a different outcome? The odds would have, of course, been stacked against Lucas.

This troubles me but gives meaning to the Mental Health Runner project.

If I had successfully taken my own life; then I couldn't have been there to help keep Lucas alive until the paramedics arrived, it could have meant the death of another.

That's what I want this project to be about.

From its conception as an idea, to its birth, in the present and in the future. I want people to know, no matter race, sexuality, location or any other diversity our planet is made up of; suicide is never the answer and there is, I promise, a way to see the light at the end of the tunnel.

It may take time and there are hardships and commitments along the way, but trust me. You will have one hell of a story to tell.

Chapter 22-Changing the conversation (A)

Tom and I now live a relatively average life. We work full time; we live with our two beautiful dogs; we take holidays and go to gigs and things are pretty good most of the time. We have had to accept that our life will always come with greater ups and downs than most couples', but we now know how to manage these. I'm in the fortunate position to have worked in Mental Health roles for several years now. This means I have a pretty good armoury of tools and strategies that I've been able to teach Tom to help him manage various aspects of his mental health. It also means I am constantly surrounded by people who I know will understand when things are difficult.

It has taken us a long time to reach this point and accept the hand that life dealt us. We agreed quite early on that we didn't just want our journey to be an awful, shameful memory, but rather, we needed to do something to make the whole experience somehow worthwhile. It seemed obvious to us that the best way to do this was to do the one thing we had avoided for so long. We needed to talk about it. To his credit, Tom well and truly took the bull by the horns and started speaking more openly about what he'd been through. I think there was some element of necessity about this as he needed certain people: family, work and friends to know and understand. However, he very quickly progressed to delivering talks at work, in schools, local business and amazingly, a TEDx talk.

As for me, I'm getting there slowly. When you care for someone with a mental illness, your caring role doesn't end when that person gets better, because you're always acutely aware that they could get worse again. I live in fear of slammed doors and raised voices because, for so many years of my life, that was always a precursor to the most terrifying experiences I have ever had. I worry about so many things. Will Tom's mental health decline again? If he does get ill, will cuts to mental health services mean there won't be help there for him? Will he try to kill himself again? What if he does kill himself one day? Daily life can be exhausting sometimes; constantly trying to maintain balance, spot early warning signs and planning for every possible eventuality. Often, this can lead to me reading too far into a minor change such as a door closing slightly louder than usual and assuming-usually wrongly-that it's happening all over again. Whilst I know that there will always be a part of me that will be hypervigilant, I am working on being able to worry less and live more in the moment.

For the first time in quite a few years, I'm learning to put myself first, look after myself and do things I enjoy.

I've finally found time to go back to university alongside my full-time job supporting people with mental health difficulties and although there's a regretful part of me that feels I should have done this much sooner; I'm so happy to finally be living my life, knowing that I don't have to worry so much about Tom in the meantime.

I'm also learning to think and talk more about my experience of Tom's illness.

I've always been aware that I'd blocked out a lot of what happened over the last few years; something, I think, I did to survive. I knew that if I dwelled too much on what was happening in the midst of it all, I would crumble, and so I spent a lot of time in autopilot just doing what needed to be done. I'm not sure that I realised until we started writing this book, however, just how much I had blocked out.

Remembering things that happened and how I felt has been an incredibly painful experience. If I close my eyes and think about certain events; I can still remember the tightening in my chest, the fear, desperation and the hopelessness of it all. It wasn't until recently that I realised that often I would talk about what happened and focus heavily on Tom, or I would talk about it in quite an emotionless and matter-of-fact way.

I've watched people cry hearing about our story and felt so disconnected from it all, that I couldn't understand what was so sad. So, a huge leap for me has been intentionally allowing myself to reconnect with my experience in an emotional way; that has been extremely cathartic and I think, allowed me to process things and move forward.

Remembering how excruciatingly alone I felt has also ignited a new fire in me.

It might sound obvious, but recently, I've realised that I was never alone, I was just invisible.

There are plenty more people like me who are supporting a loved one through mental illness; our journeys might be different, but I'd be willing to bet that we've all felt alone, scared, frustrated, and at times like we didn't know what we were doing.

For me though, I had that sense of duty: I had to keep going because how could Tom rely on me if I was struggling too?

Until that first therapist acknowledged me as a carer and made it ok to ask for help; I never knew any different. Until you become a carer, you have no reason to know what support is available or what to expect; some of us might not know there is help available and accept the new normal without question; others might know they need help but through guilt, shame or sheer lack of time and energy, not feel able to find it. I was definitely a mix of the two.

This is why I feel passionately that more needs to be done to support carers.

I can't help but think that if any one of the professionals walking through our door into the destruction and chaos, or the many we saw in A&E had stopped to ask if I needed help in supporting Tom; things might have gotten better for us sooner.

If I had been allowed into his consultation in A&E the night he tried to hang himself in our garage; I could have told them about how worried I was that he was still a risk to himself, or at least I would have known about the medication he'd been given.

Maybe then I could have stopped him from overdosing.

I was spending my life trying to keep the person I love alive, and helping him to get better, but how could I ever do that effectively if I didn't have the support, information and tools to do so? How can anyone?

Things might not have been any different, but perhaps if someone had told me that support was there, it wouldn't have taken me to be struggling so much with my own mental health for things to start to improve.

The conversation around mental health has grown tremendously in recent years, and the campaigns urging us to reach out to those in need have helped so many people, but it's not enough. We need to get better at talking more openly about mental illness and the impact it can have. As well as making it acceptable to talk about our own mental health difficulties; we need to normalise the difficulties faced by family, friends, carers or those who are struggling in order to ease the guilt felt by people like me for finding that caring role difficult. Simply by acknowledging that carers exist and that their role is tough, we can make it so much easier for them to ask for help.

So, as painful as talking about this time of our life is; I am now trying to take responsibility and do my bit to bring carers into the conversation about mental health in the hope that others will do the same. I regularly use my social media to share parts of our story that even those closest to me never knew, and have overcome my fear of judgement to talk publicly at mental health events about my experience as a carer. Every time I share this piece of my life, I do it with just one goal in mind.

Whether you are a healthcare professional, teacher, family member, friend, colleague or even acquaintance who knows someone with a mental health problem; reach out to those around them and ask if they're ok. If you know that someone close to you or someone, you're working with professionally is supporting someone with a mental health problem, offer them support, or even better, find out who the local carer support service is in your area and give them a leaflet.

If you aren't for whatever reason, in a position to help someone you care about directly; if nothing else, be patient with them. Keep inviting them for coffee; let them know that you're there when they're ready and that you still value them, even though they might be too busy to maintain your friendship right now. It really helps when, like me, you're coming out of the other side of your caring role to know that you still have friends around and a life after caring. Sometimes even just a little kindness and understanding is enough.

These are such simple things, but you have no idea what a difference they make to a carer like me.

More Information

For more information regarding mental health in the UK:

https://mind.org.uk
https://www.rethink.org
https://www.samaritans.org
Https://thecalmzone.net
https://www.runtalkrun.com/

If you or someone else is requiring urgent help, visit your nearest A&E or
call your local emergency number.

For more information, or if you'd like to contact Tom or Amber; You can also find out more here:-

https://www.instagtram.com/Mental_health_runner
https://www.instagram.com/Amber_Dunning_X
https://www.mentalhealthrunner.co.uk/
thomas@mentalhealthrunner.co.uk

Chronos Publishing

Life Stories

We sincerely hope you enjoyed this book.

If you'd like to know more about our forthcoming titles, authors and special events, or to be notified of early releases then follow us:

on Facebook @ChronosPublishing

on Twitter @ChronosPublish

or come find us on the web at:

www.chronospublishing.com

We love what we do and we'd like you to be part of a thriving community of people who enjoy books and the very best reading experiences.

Taryn Johnston
Creative Director
FCM Media Group